Saying
Goodbye
when you don't want to

Saying
Goodbye
when you don't want to

TEENS DEALING WITH LOSS

MARTHA BOLTON

SERVANT PUBLICATIONS
ANN ARBOR, MICHIGAN

Vine Books is an imprint of Servant Publications especially designed to serve
Evangelical Christians.

Published by Servant Publications
P.O. Box 8617
Ann Arbor, Michigan 48107

Cover design: Uttley/Douponce DesignWorks, Sisters, Oregon

02 03 04 05 10 9 8 7 6 5 4 3 2 1

Printed in the United States of America
ISBN 1-56955-266-5

Library of Congress Cataloging-in-Publication Data

Bolton, Martha, 1951-
    Saying good-bye when you don't want to : teens dealing with loss /
Martha Bolton.
        p. cm.
    Summary: Uses personal experiences, poetry, and Scripture verses to provide
advice on how to cope with all kinds of loss in one's life, including death, moving, the end of a friendship, and other difficult situations.
    ISBN 1-56955-266-5 (alk. paper)
    1. Consolaton—Juvenile literature. 2. Bereavement—Religious aspects—
Christianity—Juvenile literature. 3. Grief—Religious aspects—Christianity—
Juvenile literature. 4. Death—Religious aspects—Christianity—Juvenile literature. [1. Loss (Psychology) —Religious aspects—Christianity. 2. Grief—Religious
aspects—Christianity.] I. Title.
    BV4905.3 .B65 2002
    248.8'6—dc21
                                                                    2001007128

In memory of Anne Farris

"Good people will be remembered as a blessing."

PROVERBS 10:7

Contents

Foreword

Being a teenager can be pretty puzzling. It's a time of hopes and dreams, disappointments and losses and, with any luck at all, a new understanding of self. It's a teenager's job to develop his or her own identity. This is a necessary developmental stage, often as tumultuous as the "terrible twos." At two, you expected your parents to be around to handle life's complications for you. But by the time you have reached your teenage years, you've no doubt felt the sting of a few complications yourself. You may have had to say goodbye to some things or people to whom you weren't prepared to say goodbye, or perhaps you've made a few poor choices along the way to adulthood. Yet that's what growing up is. It's taking chances and making choices. It's learning from both your right decisions and your not-so-right ones. It's loving, even at the risk of having to let go. It's asking yourself a lot of questions: Will this behavior fit my personality? Will these friends echo what is important to me? Is this what I want to be when I grow up? Will my parents still love me if I begin to declare some independence? Will they catch me when I start to fall? Do these friends fit well enough to trust? It's a lot like trying on new outfits at the mall. So many look inviting. Sometimes you find just the right fit, yet sometimes, discouragingly, nothing seems to fit at all.

You may even find yourself asking God a few questions: Why did this have to happen to me? Why did my father have to die? Why did my family have to move? Why did my boyfriend and I have to break up?

Martha has assembled a book of hope, interspersing the voices of teens across the country with her own wit and style. Readers of this book will find company and reassurance in the survival of others through the roller-coaster experiences of these often confusing years.

It has been my honor to call Martha a friend for many years, even through the raising of our own teenagers. We have shared the heartache and newfound knowledge of many disappointments and losses over the years. Through all of this, Martha has never lost her graceful way of caring, her sense of humor, or her faith in God. She has been an inspiration to me and, without a doubt, will be to you as well.

Linda Aleahmad, MA, LMFT

Acknowledgments

A special thanks

—to all the wonderful people at Vine Books/Servant Publications, but most especially Sandy Judd, Heidi Saxton, Kathy Deering, and Amy Deardorff for all their hard work in helping to make this book come together. I could not have completed it without you! You're terrific!

—to everyone who helped with this book in any way, and a very special thanks to Diantha Ain and Linda Aleahmad for their contributions and cherished friendship.

—to my husband, whose love and support have divided the pain of our own personal losses and multiplied the joy of our many blessings.

—to Russ II, Matt, Nicole, Tony, Crystal, and Kiana, who top that list of blessings.

—and to the hundreds of you who sent me stories for this book. I wish I could have included each one of them! May God continue to heal the pain of your losses, and may you find comfort in your beloved memories, His love, and the love and encouragement of those around you.

Martha Bolton

Preface

The letter was from Maria Billings Schneider of Georgia. She explained that she was the aunt of *Brio* magazine reader Anne Farris. Maria was putting together a booklet to present to her niece Anne on her upcoming birthday, and she was asking different people to write down their secret to success so she could include it in the booklet.

Apparently, Anne was a fan of The Cafeteria Lady, a column I write for *Brio*, and she had several of the youth devotionals that I have written. So Maria included me in her list of contributors to Anne's booklet.

I answered the question, but for some reason I felt like I should take a little more time with my response than I normally would. Anne had to have been pretty special for her aunt to do such a thoughtful thing for her.

What I told Anne, basically, was that the secret to success is knowing that you're in the will of God. Everything else in life is secondary.

A few months passed and I didn't think any more about it until one day a letter from Anne arrived in the mail. It was a beautiful letter, thanking me for sharing in her aunt's gift, and saying that what I had written had really encouraged her. I was touched, and it verified for me that I had done the right thing when I took the extra time for my response.

As I tried to put the letter back into the envelope, I noticed there was something else in there. I reached in and took it out. It was a newspaper clipping of Anne Farris' obituary. I read it, then reread it, then checked the name on the letter. They were the same. The article said that Anne Farris had collapsed and died suddenly while running a lap. Apparently, Anne had written the thank-you letter before her passing, and her mother, Raynette Billings Farris, had decided to go ahead and mail it to me.

My eyes filled with tears and my hands trembled as I held Anne's letter and looked again at the beautiful young girl pictured in the obituary. Elizabeth Anne Farris was only fourteen years old. She was a ninth-grade student at Oconee County High School, and a member of the Fellowship of Christian Athletes.

I wrote to Anne's mother, expressing my sympathy for the loss of her only child and best friend. In her response letter, she mentioned that since so many of Anne's friends were having to deal with overwhelming feelings of grief and shock, she wondered if I had ever thought of writing a book for teenagers dealing with the death of a friend.

Hence, this book was born. We have broadened it to include other kinds of losses that teens sometimes have to deal with in life—the loss of a parent, grandparent, or sibling, the loss of a relationship, the loss of familiar surroundings, surviving divorce, and even the loss of a pet.

If you're a hurting teen, or you know someone who has recently suffered a loss, we pray this book will be an encouragement. And if, from this book, you come to understand that you are not alone in your grief, that the feelings you are experiencing right now are perfectly normal, that there is hope to be grasped, and that one day you will smile again, then we've done what we set out to do.

Martha Bolton

CHAPTER 1

Saying Goodbye to a Friend

There is a time for everything, and a season for every activity under heaven: a time to be born and a time to die, a time to plant and a time to uproot.

ECCLESIASTES 3:1,2

It's never easy to say goodbye to a friend. Maybe that's because friends are people who are in our lives by invitation. No one's forcing us to like them, or them us. We just do. Perhaps it's their sense of humor that originally drew us to them, or their love of adventure, or maybe it's the fact that they're good listeners and can be trusted with our confidences. No matter what the driving force was behind their formation, friendships have been established, and in some instances, we may even feel closer to that friend than we do to our own brothers or sisters.

Having to say goodbye to someone like that isn't easy. Sure, we can form new friendships, but the vacuum left behind by the death of a good friend may never be fully filled.

Understanding the whys behind the goodbyes can be difficult, too. You were just with your friend yesterday at school. Or last night at church. Or you went to the mall with him or her last week. Why didn't you see it coming? Why wasn't there some warning? Why did this have to happen to your friend? This friend?

When my son was about ten years old, one of his good friends, someone who played at our house frequently, died suddenly one night. He had some sort of heart malfunction at his home during the night and later died in the hospital. It was a shock to the whole neighborhood. He was buried in his Little League uniform, and needless to say, the neighborhood was depressingly quiet for many months after that.

There was no way for my son to have known his friend was going to die that night. Ten-year-old friends aren't supposed to die. Neither are fifteen-year-old friends. Or thirty-year-old friends. If you are blessed with a long life, chances are you'll outlive a lot of friends. People in their seventies and eighties usually have more friends and family on the other side than they have here in this life. Maybe that's one of the things that's going to make heaven so much fun. It'll be a grand reunion with the friends we've lost from childhood, our teenage years, and all the years afterward. And although to us it may seem like decades before we will be able to run up to them and deliver that long-awaited hug, to them, it'll be just the blink of an eye.

When It Takes You by Surprise

I looked down the church hall to see twelve-year-old Danielle laughing as always and playing with her young cousins. Her identical twin sister, Andrea, was standing next to her, laughing too. Almost no one could tell the twins apart, but I could. I had known them for a long time and felt a special friendship with each one of them.

Danielle and I didn't really get a chance to talk that Sunday, but I thought nothing of it. There was always next week, right? I didn't know that would be the last time I would see Danielle alive.

About midweek, Danielle began to feel very sick and started running a fever. At first, it didn't appear to be anything more serious than a passing virus, but when her condition worsened, Danielle was rushed to the hospital. A preliminary examination didn't reveal the origin of the pain, but as a precaution, the doctors felt that Danielle should remain in the hospital overnight. The question many kept asking was whether or not it could be appendicitis, but the answer was always no.

The doctors gave Danielle a medication to flush out her system, but soon after, disaster struck. Danielle's temperature soared to 106 degrees. Immediately, they packed her in ice in an effort to bring down the fever, then later transferred her to a larger, better equipped hospital for treatment. My dad, the pastor of our church, prayed over her. That's all any of us could do—pray.

Friday night our church youth group was scheduled to have its annual Christmas party, but none of us felt in the festive spirit. We basically just sat around and awaited word about Danielle. Word came that she had to undergo an emergency operation. During the operation it was discovered that her appendix had indeed ruptured. Danielle miraculously survived the operation, but she still wasn't out of danger.

Later that next week, I came home and noticed my dad sitting by the computer, e-mailing a prayer request. When I asked what was wrong, he told me that Danielle had taken a turn for the worse. Fear gripped my heart. I went into my room and prayed. It all seemed so unreal.

Danielle was now on life support. I went on the Internet to

e-mail my friends to pray for her, even the ones who had no clue who she was. When the telephone rang that day, I got a sick feeling in the pit of my stomach. Hesitantly, I picked up the phone. My friend Kristin said only two words, words that would change my life forever.

"She died."

I dreaded going to the hospital that day. My mother had succumbed to cancer just a little over a year before, and I hated hospitals. But I knew I had to be strong to help Andrea get through this.

I miss my friend Danielle, but her death has taught me something about life. We don't know when someone we love is going to be taken from us. We especially don't expect someone so young, so healthy, so in love with life to leave us, but Danielle did. Even though she had gone to be with the Lord, it still bothered me that I didn't get a chance to say goodbye. One week she was alive and laughing, the next week she was fighting for her life. I had the time. I could have talked with her that day. I could have given her one last hug. I could have assured her once again of my friendship and love. But I didn't know it would be the last time I saw her. I just didn't know.

Stephanie Bernotas
Age 13

Out of our anguish
arises an inner strength
we've not known before.

Haiku by Diantha Ain

As you walk through the valley of the unknown, you will
find the footprints of Jesus both in front of you and
beside you.

Charles Stanley

When You Can't Understand Why

Dear Greg,

We never got to know each other very well. Now I regret not
pursuing our friendship sooner, because our chance for that
friendship is now gone forever.

It all started right before Christmas break of 1999, which
seems so far away right now. We were told that you had been
diagnosed with leukemia. As the word quickly spread, we were
all in tears, worrying about you, and hoping and praying that
you would beat the life-threatening disease.

Our teachers told us you were going to be fine, that the
leukemia was curable and that you would be back to school
soon. We believed them, and trusted that everything was going
to work itself out.

Still, we prayed. And hoped. I prayed every night for you and
your family. I remember asking God to let me know, or even
give me the slightest hint, as to why you had to go through this
time of trial. You were such a great guy. Great guys and girls
shouldn't have to fight for their lives.

I received a phone call from my best friend the night you passed
away. She called at an unusual time, so naturally I wondered
what was wrong. She told me you had moved on to a better

place. I was in so much shock I didn't know what to say. I wasn't expecting it. The teachers had said you were going to be OK. None of us expected you to die.

Going to school the following day was probably the hardest thing I've ever had to do. I think the whole school was in shock. Classes were held, but no one could concentrate. We all spent the day grieving and comforting each other. Now that you are gone, I believe God has answered my question as to why you had to suffer. Greg, you have no idea how many people your life and death have impacted, mine definitely being one of them. You were an amazing guy and a role model for all of us. We're committed to following your example. Also, because of your death, the kids at our high school have become better friends to each other. It was you who brought us together!

Aileen Nosal

Out of suffering have emerged the strongest souls.
Edwin Hubbel Chapin

Anne

Her first time skating.
And her last.
Picture perfect
until my eyes fill with tears.
Her hair, blonde,
eyes baby blue.
Silver skates hit the ice
and she glides
to the pathway where the big man awaits.

Into the light,
her soul flies,
leaving us struggling to keep our balance
on this cold, slippery circle of life.
But the memory
of her laughter
warms our hearts
as it always has.
The picture turns
one last time,
taking her to the top of the frame,
where she peeks out from the clouds.
I can see her smile.
She likes the view.
I know now that she's okay.
And so am I.

Brooke Faulkner
In memory of Anne Farris

To live in hearts we leave behind is not to die.

Clyde Campbell

When You Learn More Than You Realize

Monday, May 3, 1999. The day that changed Big Rapids High School forever.

When I got on the bus that morning, a fellow classmate told me that Mr. DeCoster had died on Sunday in a house fire in Grand Haven. Bret A. DeCoster was twenty-three years old and a first-year teacher at B.R.H.S. He was the varsity soccer coach and the junior class advisor.

But Mr. DeCoster was more than a teacher. He was more than a coach. He was "Mr. D." He was "D." He was "Zero." His nicknames were as warm and friendly as he was. Mr. D. was someone to whom you could relate. You could talk to him about anything, and he was never too busy to listen.

Mr. D. was always making us laugh, too. His cheerful grin remained constant, no matter what, and he loved to joke around. He loved suckers, too. We hardly ever saw him without a sucker in his mouth.

Two hundred and twenty-five students and staff went to his funeral, and many of us signed a banner as our way of saying goodbye. Teachers and students also shared funny memories of Mr. D. to help bring closure to this unfortunate tragedy.

In the short time that Mr. D. was at B.R.H.S., he bonded with and won the hearts of many students. It's not often that teens find such a positive role model who gives as much as he receives.

Things will never be the same at Big Rapids High School. This was the closest many of us students had ever been to death, and it forced us to grow up in so many ways. We all miss Mr. DeCoster a lot. But I, for one, will be forever thankful to a teacher who did more than just teach us from books. Mr. DeCoster taught us about life, about attitude, and especially about laughter.

Jill Duran
In loving memory of Bret DeCoster

Great beginnings are not as important as the way one finishes.

Dr. James Dobson

A Step Toward Healing

If you've recently lost a friend, write down three reasons why you feel blessed to have had this person in your life.

In what way could you use this loss to help others?

Chapter 2

Saying Goodbye to a Sibling

The Lord gives strength to his people; the Lord blesses his people with peace.

PSALM 29:11

It's difficult to say goodbye to someone with whom you've laughed, cried, done chores, avoided chores, gotten grounded, played games, gone to church, done homework, gone on vacations, watched television, played video games, and shared just about every other activity you can think of. This is someone who will always be a part of your life. When you look through family albums, you'll remember him. When you share memories over dinner, she'll be a part of them.

Losing a sibling is difficult on another level as well. When you lose a friend, your family can be there to help get you through it. When you lose a sibling, however, your whole family is feeling the loss, so there might not be enough encouragement to go around. You could find yourself feeling alone in your grief, while others are busy consoling your parents.

If you find yourself in a situation like this, you need to reach out and let someone know you're hurting. Too often adults believe the brave face that teenagers are well practiced at putting on, the face that says "everything's fine, I can handle it," when nothing's fine and you're about to fall apart. It's all right to ask for help. It's all right to talk about your loss, even if you get angry, or cry, or dare to ask God why. It's healthy, and it's how you begin to heal.

When You Didn't Get the Chance to Say Goodbye

When they wheeled my brother out of the doctor's office and into the ambulance, he was in shock and somewhat delirious. He looked at me and said one word, "Coke."

I almost smiled. It was his favorite drink. I had no idea that one word would be the last one he would ever say to me. By morning he was gone. A viral pneumonia had taken over his lungs, and sometime during the night, he quietly slipped away from me.

Brothers aren't supposed to die so young. They're supposed to grow up and grow old with you. Even if you're not that close, you just kind of take it for granted that they'll always be there. So, for me, the hardest part of saying goodbye was not ever getting the chance to say it.

When someone you love dies unexpectedly, a lot of things are left unsaid. You think of all the stories you forgot to tell that person, the apologies you wanted to make but never got around to, the jokes you meant to tell, and the "I love you's" you wanted to say, but figured you'd do tomorrow.

On the day of my brother's funeral, all my good intentions lay like jagged steppingstones on the path to his gravesite. There was so much I had wanted to say to him, but that wasn't an option anymore. So, I did the only thing I could do that day—

I said goodbye to a body. I never said goodbye to my brother.

Over and over, I've asked God why. Why did my brother have to die? I do know this—my brother carried some pretty heavy loads while he was here. Like a mismatched puzzle, the pieces of his life just never seemed to fit together. I think maybe now they finally do. I also know that whatever heartaches or troubles my brother experienced here on earth, they're now over. He is, at last, at peace. Whenever I think about him, I feel a little part of that peace, even in my tears.

No, I never had the chance to say good-bye to my brother, or to tell him one last time that I loved him. Yet in a way, I've never stopped saying it. I say it when I hear one of his favorite songs, hear a really bad pun (he loved puns), or look into the faces of his son and daughter.

Goodbye, Dickie, be at rest. I love you.

Sandy Brownlee
Writer/Radio personality

I wanted a perfect ending. Now I've learned, the hard way, that some poems don't rhyme, and some stories don't have a clear beginning, middle, and end. Life is about not knowing, having to change, taking the moment and making the best of it without knowing what's going to happen next.

Gilda Radner
Comedian

When the Laughter Doesn't Help

The doctor came in and explained as best he could to my fifteen-year-old sister Cheralyn about leukemia, how it works, and how they would be fighting it. Cheralyn nodded as if to say, "I understand," then boldly asked the doctor, "Am I going to die?"

The doctor was honest and said, "Right now there is a greater chance that you will."

It had been less than two years since we had lost my other sister, Charlotta, in a fatal car accident, and since her death I had grown closer to Cheralyn. Sometimes I'd lie in bed with her and watch TV. I'd read all the get-well cards to her (there were scores), and she'd tell me where she wanted them taped to the wall. Sometimes I'd help her wash her hair and comb it just right.

After two weeks in the hospital, two weeks of not getting much better, Cheralyn took a turn for the worse, and the doctors frantically searched for a bone marrow donor. We were ecstatic when my brother Mike turned out to be a perfect match.

It was late Sunday night when I kissed Cheralyn good night. I didn't dare to say goodbye. I'd already said a few too many of those in my short life. Besides, there was that bone marrow transplant scheduled for Monday, so there was hope.

I remember pulling the door closed quietly and catching one last glimpse of Cheralyn's eyes as Mother settled in the chair next to her bed. Mom opened the Bible and began to read the verses that Cheralyn loved to hear again and again: "Therefore we do not lose heart. Though outwardly we are wasting away, yet inwardly we are being renewed day by day.... So we fix our eyes not on what is seen, but what is unseen. For what is seen is temporary, but what is unseen is eternal" (2 Cor 4:16-18).

On Monday morning, the day when the bone marrow transplant was scheduled to take place, Cheralyn slipped away from us, and there was nothing we could do about it.

Something else slipped away from me that day, too: laughter. No matter how often I had been able to make Cheralyn laugh, that laughter had not done her "good like a medicine." Or me. I couldn't hear it anymore. Neither did I want to. The grief was too dark, too loud. Sometimes grief rings so loudly in your ears that you just can't hear anything else. And now the laughter hurt. I couldn't see how I would ever laugh again.

So much time has gone by now that the majority of my life has been spent without my sisters in it. I still feel that incredible sinking feeling whenever I think of sitting there in that funeral home chair—or when I smell freshly turned earth. Yet I've learned to live with it, work around it, move on, plunge through it. (The more verbs the better.)

And I have somehow learned, even though I would not have believed it possible at the time, that I can truly laugh again. A healthy laugh, from a healthy place.

Chonda Pierce
Comedian

Those who don't know how to weep with their whole heart don't know how to laugh either.

Golda Meir

When a Phone Call Changes Your Life

I was at home, watching a movie, when the phone call came that would change my life forever. Routinely, I set the movie on *pause* and picked up the receiver.

"Hello?" I answered.

"Do you know a Jesse Carlson?" said the person on the other end of the line.

"He's my brother," I said, guardedly. "Why do you ask?"

"Is your mother or father home?"

"No, they're at a movie. What's wrong?"

"There's been an ... an accident."

The stranger on the phone went on to explain that my brother had been hit by a car and was in critical condition.

The movie theater was close to my house, so I hung up the phone and walked there. Make that "ran there." I told the ticket taker that there was a family emergency, and he went inside and found my parents. When they came out, I told them.

"Jesse's in the hospital."

That was all I needed to say. We got in the car and raced to the hospital. When we walked into my brother's room, I froze. I had planned on talking to him, but I just couldn't. He looked so helpless lying there. He didn't look like my brother at all.

I turned away and sat on the bench outside his room in shock. When it came time for us to leave, I heard my parents tell him goodbye and promise to see him the next day. Then I overheard the doctor telling my parents, "I'm not saying it'll happen, but there's a possibility that your son may go into a coma. If you're lucky, he'll be out of here within two weeks."

My other siblings and I all slept in my room that night in

sleeping bags. We played the music as loudly as we could, into the middle of the night, in a futile effort to drown out our thoughts and fears of what still could happen.

After we stayed up all night talking, purposely avoiding the subject of our brother, our parents woke us up early the next day to tell us they were going to the hospital.

My younger sister was too young to visit the Critical Condition ward, so she went to my grandparents' home, while the rest of us went to see Jesse. This time, I was determined not to let my fear keep me from talking to him.

My parents went in first, and of course they talked for awhile. I waited on the bench with my brother, but neither of us talked. I think we were too scared to talk about Jesse. When my parents came out, it was my turn.

I walked into Jesse's room and found him lying there, bruised and scraped up and looking very weak. I took a deep breath and tried to look cheerful and confident.

"Hey, Jess," I said.

"Hey, Tori," he said, trying his best to give me a smile.

There was silence for a few minutes. I wanted to talk, but couldn't let him hear the fear in my voice, so I just sat there looking into his brown eyes. They were so innocent and reflected his personality—strong, compassionate, full of life. I knew I had to remember this moment.

"Tori, listen to me," he began. "I love you and I don't want to die...."

"Don't talk like that!" I said.

"Let me finish," he said, determined to share what was on his heart. "If I do die, then I want you to be careful. Take care of yourself and of our brothers and sisters. OK?"

I nodded, trying my best to hold back the tears.

"Don't cry, Tori," he said in his big brother voice. "Do not cry."

"I won't," I promised.

Just then the nurse came in and told me that my time was up. Jess reached his arms out for a hug. As I hugged him, a quote I once heard came to me, "Hug someone a little tighter today, you might not get the chance tomorrow." I hugged my brother a little tighter.

That night I was very edgy. I didn't want to talk to anyone, and I tried my best not to think about my brother.

When the phone rang during the night, a chill went through me. I could tell by the tone of my mother's voice that the news wasn't good.

"Is Jesse in a coma?" I asked as soon as she hung up the telephone.

"No, sweetie," she said, then called my father into another room to talk. After a few moments, they called all of us kids into the room.

"Kids, I have to ..." my mother started.

"Is it about Jesse?" my brother asked.

"I have to talk to you about your brother. I guess a few minutes ago he was having trouble," she said, taking a deep breath before continuing. "He checked out of the hospital. He had a better offer up in heaven."

All I could think of was that this was some kind of a sick joke.

"THAT IS SO NOT FUNNY!" I yelled.

"Honey, I wish I was joking," my mom said, tears streaming down her cheeks.

"Jesse's gone?" asked my little sister, quietly.

I left the room and went on a bike ride. I tried to avoid my brother's route, and as much as I tried not to, I thought of him. I stopped at the hospital and went in to ask if I could see my brother's room one last time. To my surprise, they let me. When I reached his room, though, the nurses were in there, preparing to take him out. I couldn't see Jess dead. I just couldn't. So I sat on the bench. I sat there for almost an hour before one of the hospital staff asked me to leave. Confused and angry, I rolled my eyes and walked out of the hospital.

Everything was happening so fast, and I didn't know how to process it in my mind. I still hadn't cried. I didn't want to, because that would make it real. As long as I didn't cry, didn't feel, then maybe it wasn't true. Maybe Jess was still here. I can't explain the emptiness I felt inside. I began to rebel. Each time I walked past Jess' room at our house, I felt like I couldn't live through another day without him.

Finally, I had a talk with my pastor and he told me that I needed to make Jess' death real. I couldn't keep running away from reality. Not acknowledging Jess' death wouldn't bring him back, but facing it, getting angry about it, crying over the loss, and eventually accepting it was all part of the healing process. That night, I cried myself to sleep.

When I woke up the next morning, a miracle hadn't taken all the pain away, but I did feel better. And now, a year later, whenever someone asks if I still miss him, I say, "Of course, I miss him." I'll always miss him. But you know when you get a burn or a scratch? It hurts at first, but after awhile the pain goes away. Still, it leaves a mark. That's how it is with Jesse. The wound of his death has healed, but the scar is still there, as well as the memories. He taught me so much. And I'm so glad I listened to my heart that night in the hospital room and hugged him just a little bit tighter.

Natalie
(as told to Hope Stowe)

Do not grieve, for the joy of the Lord is your strength.
NEHEMIAH 8:10

When You Wish You Could Change the World

If I could change one thing about the world today, it would be that someone would find a cure for cancer, so that families would not have to go through what mine has gone through over the past two years. Last fall, my fourteen-year-old brother Matt died of cancer. Since we are only eighteen months apart, we've always been very close. When I was younger, I wouldn't go anywhere without him. Throughout our lives, we shared jokes, laughter, secrets, and more. We were not just brother and sister; we were good friends.

In September 1998, Matt and I both had new teachers at school, and while we were expecting exciting things in our junior high years, we certainly were not expecting something that was to change our lives forever.

After school one day, my friend's mom picked me up. I assumed it was because my mother had taken Matt to the doctor to find out why some lymph nodes on his neck were swollen. When my mom called to tell me that they had discovered Matt had leukemia (cancer of the blood), I was in complete shock. My first thought was, "Is Matt going to die?" Then I was afraid.

Nothing of this magnitude had ever happened to me, and it shouldn't be happening to someone just starting the sixth grade. I didn't know what to do. I spent that first night at my neighbor's house, crying silently into my pillow.

The next few months were a blur of endless nights at the hospital. Due to radiation and chemotherapy, Matt's hair fell out and he began to lose weight and strength. Yet no matter how different he appeared on the outside, I knew that he was the same Matt inside, my same loving, caring older brother.

A year after treatment, Matt had a relapse. Although it was risky, doctors determined that the best option for Matt to regain his health was a bone marrow transplant. A bone marrow transplant is a procedure where the marrow of a healthy person (a sibling is best) is infused into the body of the patient to replace the diseased cells with healthy cells, hopefully arresting the cancer.

I went with my older half-siblings to be tested, and when I learned I was a perfect match, I was excited to possibly be the means for Matt's recovery. The procedure extracted marrow from my hipbone, and while it required me to be in the hospital for three days, Matt ended up being in the hospital for four months.

Since my parents were with Matt 24/7, I stayed with my friend, Laura Fresch, and her family for those four months. They were all so nice, but it was certainly a new and different experience for me to live apart from my family.

After Matt's transplant, it was pretty much smooth sailing. Matt began to get his life back. His hair grew in, and in June he was a speaker at his eighth-grade graduation. He even got to enjoy the summer, going to camp, traveling to Wisconsin, attending summer school to prepare him for Loyola High School, and hanging out with his friends.

Sadly, though, after his first week at Loyola, Matt suffered another relapse of his cancer. This time, in spite of the best medical treatment, the cancer persisted, and Matt was given a devastating prognosis. The doctors told us that Matt might live anywhere from two days to two years. We had Matt for barely two months.

We didn't waste a minute. Every single day of those final months, we told Matt we loved him. We even took him on a Disney cruise, only to have him airlifted off the ship to a Florida hospital. In the Pediatric Intensive Care Unit of the Miami Children's Hospital, I talked to Matt for hours, and even though he couldn't talk back, I knew he understood what I was saying. I sang songs to him, and on November 10, I had to say goodbye to my beloved brother. It was the hardest thing I've ever done, but I will always have happy memories of us at camp, playing soccer, going on trips, or just playing a game of Monopoly.

Although my brother's cancer was a horrible thing, there were a number of good things that came out of his illness. Friends, neighbors, and even strangers showed us their love by bringing meals, helping with transportation and expenses, taking care of our house and dog, staying at the hospital with us, sponsoring a golf tournament in Matt's name, and even running a blood drive. Religious groups near and far joined together and prayed constantly for us. So many things were done to help us that it's hard to list them all. And Matt's positive attitude through it all showed us how to cherish life and make the best of every day, even if your life doesn't turn out to be what you expected it to be. Matt focused on what he could do, not what he couldn't, and lived his life to the fullest. While he always knew the reality of his illness, he didn't dwell on anything but his full recovery. I miss Matt a lot, but I know he still is, and always will be, my brother, and I also know that even now he's watching over me.

If I could change one thing about the world, it would be that someone would find a cure for cancer. Cancer is a horrible and life-threatening disease. Most of us have been affected by it in some way. If a cure could be found, children and teenagers and cancer victims of all ages wouldn't have to die prematurely.

I cannot help but wonder what a difference these people could have made in the world. I know Matt would have made a difference. But then again, he already has.

Megan Johnson
Age 14

For he does not willingly bring affliction or grief to the children of men.

LAMENTATIONS 3:33

No sorrow touches man until it has been filtered through the heart of God.

Joseph D. Blinco

A Step Toward Healing

If you've lost a sister or brother, in what ways do you think you could honor his or her life?

Recall a funny memory of your sibling, and when you feel you're ready, share it with someone.

Chapter 3

Saying Goodbye to Familiar Surroundings

Surely I am with you always, to the very end of the age.
MATTHEW 28:10

Have you ever heard the saying, "Home is where the heart is"? It's been printed on parchment, embroidered on pillows, and silk-screened on T-shirts. I think I even wrote it on a cake once, but it was difficult to read through all the smoke. Still, there's a lot of truth in that saying. No matter where your physical body happens to be, home to you will always be that place that's home in your heart.

My family and I lived for over two decades in a small track house in Southern California. It was the only home I ever knew, growing up. But "home" to my parents was always Arkansas. When we'd visit there every summer, we weren't going on vacation to Arkansas, we were going "home."

I stayed in California for many years, until a move to Tennessee a few years ago. It was a difficult move for a lot of different reasons, but now our new state is beginning to feel like home to us. I still have some family in California, and many beloved friends, and of course I miss them, but we've kept in touch. That's one good thing about the Internet. You can easily stay in contact with people, whether they're across the street or across the country. The print doesn't get any smaller because of distance. In fact, since moving to Tennessee, I've talked to some friends through e-mail a lot more than I ever got to talk to them in person in California.

In writing this book, I've received hundreds of e-mails from teens all over the world. Many were from different places here in the United States, but some were from as far away as Australia, Singapore, England, Romania, and other distant locales. And you know what? If they hadn't said in their e-mails where they were writing from, I wouldn't ever have known the difference.

So, if you're facing a difficult move, remember to look at it as an adventure. My nephew made a reluctant move with his family, but ended up meeting the president of the United States after helping out with a weather disaster near his new home. You just never know what adventures could be in store for you.

Whether you wanted it or not, your world is expanding. Instead of resisting that change, embrace it. Go with an open heart and mind. Be friendly and you'll make new friends. Enjoy your new surroundings. Nothing says that the move has to be permanent. But it's where you'll be for right now. Make the best of it. And keep in touch with your old friends, too, because in life there's no limit to how many friends you can collect.

When New Seems Scary

My fear has always been to move. I don't like starting over. It's scary and it hurts to pull up your life from a place where everything seems to be going fine and move it to a new place where there are so many unknowns. But that's exactly what I was being asked to do, even if it was just three hundred miles away.

Beginning in August 2000, my dad became dissatisfied with his job in Knoxville, Tennessee. Another company in Brentwood, Tennessee, contacted him and asked him to head up their health care group. My sister and I have moved four times since we were small, so we were adamantly opposed to yet another relocation. I expressed that dissatisfaction by crying the entire way to Brentwood and back when my family drove there to check out the new job.

On August 16, my dad took the job with the new company. I was angry, scared, and lonely. I wasn't allowed to tell anyone, so basically I could share my feelings with only my mom or my sister. I just "knew" that this move wasn't of God. How could it be when I was so miserable?

In September, my dad moved to Brentwood to begin this new chapter in his career, while my mom, my sister, and I stayed behind in Knoxville to sell the house. When the time came for me to tell my friends the "secret" of our move, they were as devastated as I was. It helped that some of them wrote encouraging letters, gave me long hugs, and offered to pray for me.

A couple of us decided that we wanted the last few months to be full of memories, so we went practically everywhere together. It was really difficult to think of living my life away from these close friends. It had been only two years since we had moved to Knoxville, but I wouldn't trade the friends I met there for anything in the world. They were what I had always imagined best friends could be like.

Reluctantly, I counted the days until our moving date. I waited and prayed our plans would change. Of course, I wanted my family to be reunited, but I wanted to stay in Knoxville in my comfort zone even more.

On January 5, we sold our home. It was time to move, but surprisingly, the pain didn't seem to be so bad anymore. I had been memorizing Jeremiah 29:11, which says: "'For I know the plans I have for you,' declares the Lord, 'plans to prosper you, and not harm you; plans to give you a future and a hope.'" This verse encouraged me to place my full trust in God because He, above all else, knew what He was doing. On March 1, we loaded up our belongings and moved away from Knoxville. I still cried over how much I was losing, but found comfort in how much I wasn't. I was losing my comfort zone. That's all. I wasn't losing my friends.

Now I'm here in the Franklin/Brentwood area and have been for the past three months. My walk with Christ has deepened, and so have my family relationships. I still miss my Knoxville friends, and still communicate with them, but I've made some new friends here, and I've also seen some doors open that might never have opened for me, had I stayed in my comfort zone.

Being uprooted and moved three, three hundred, or even three thousand miles away is hard, really hard, but I've learned to place my trust in God, knowing the changes I face through His will won't harm me but will prosper me and give me a future and a hope.

Emily Siren
Age 14

God constantly tests
our ability to cope
with life's transitions.

Haiku by Diantha Ain

When Life Takes You to Unexpected Places

I grew up on a farm of three hundred acres. We raised cattle for beef. I always had a wonderful appreciation of the outdoors, spending most of my time working in the fields, walking in the woods, or fishing in the creeks. All of my grandparents lived nearby, so I spent a lot of time at their homes, playing with cousins and enjoying the many activities that extended families share. Sounds great, huh? Like a perfect little world? Well, it was. But all that comfort almost became a crutch to me. Of course, I didn't see it then, not when I was inside the safety of the bubble. I was just a kid having fun and growing up. One day, however, my bubble broke.

My parents weren't wealthy, so I had to fund my own way to college by pursuing loans, scholarships, work-study programs, and anything else I could think of. Somehow, I ended up in an ROTC class and eventually applied for, and received, a scholarship with them. It was a full four-year ride with a monthly stipend attached. It was definitely an answer to prayer ... or so it seemed on the surface. I was excited about the check, but I suppose it never really occurred to me that I would have to actually go into the army once I graduated from college.

Throughout my four years of schooling, I lived at home and continued to enjoy the farm, the family, the food, and the freedom.

Eventually, though, the time came to pay my dues, and my first duty assignment was Fort Lewis, Washington ... three thousand miles away from home! I was twenty-two years old and now I was heading away from home for the very first time in my life!

The trip across the United States was perhaps the lowest point in my life. Part of me was excited about starting a life of my own, but breaking away was painful. The first six months of my military experience only accented the aloneness that I felt. I was frightened. I was homesick. I was wondering what in the world I had gotten myself into.

One morning while reading a devotional, a very simple "thought for the day" struck a chord with me and became my motto for life. "Change, indeed, is painful, yet ever needful." It wasn't very profound or poetic, and I honestly can't even remember who wrote it so I can give it a proper reference. Yet that truth stuck. When I woke up in the morning, I would recite it. I wrote it down on posters and taped them to my refrigerator and to the bathroom mirror. I made placards and placed them on the desk in my office. I wrote that phrase everywhere.

After my first six months of duty, I was able to fly back to my beloved home. Then it was back to Fort Lewis, then six months later, another trip home. Each time I returned home, I felt a little different. My world was expanding in so many ways. I was working with people who were different from me—different in their life experiences, different in their backgrounds, different in their lifestyles. Home was becoming less of a safety net and more of a respite in my adventure called life.

Today, because of my career, I get on a plane and fly somewhere different every weekend. I just got back from South

Africa. In a few weeks, I'll fly to Hawaii, then back to the West Coast. I live in Virginia with my family of four. Occasionally, we get in the car and head to that place where I grew up. I no longer refer to it as "home." As my world has gotten bigger, that world has become increasingly smaller. I often wonder how I would have ended up, had it not been for the circumstances that transpired in my life, the ones that forced me into the military. I believe I'm a better person and that my life experiences have been richer because of the changes that moved me away from my comfort zone. Saying good-bye to a familiar, comfortable place in your life can sometimes mean saying hello to people, places, and experiences you never could have imagined. "Change, indeed, is painful, yet ever needful."

Jeff Smith
Playwright, actor

Reunions bring joy,
if we learn through passing time
to accept changes.

Haiku by Diantha Ain

When a Promotion Causes Commotion

In grade school and junior high, I was the kid everyone picked on. At least it seemed that way. I'd never had a really close friend, and the kids at school who I thought were my friends often were just using me to get something else; they weren't really interested in me.

After the seventh grade, my parents decided to take me out

of public school and home school me instead. We got involved with a fine arts education program and a support group for home-schoolers, and I felt like I had found my "home" at last. For the first time in my life, I felt accepted and welcomed for who I was. The other kids in the group talked to me, and we laughed together and generally had a great time. I loved every minute of my new life!

Then a bomb dropped into my world when my parents told me that my dad had been offered a promotion with his company, and it meant we would be leaving Kansas City and moving to New York. I was devastated! Everything that I had wanted in my life, and finally had gotten, was taken away in a heartbeat! Not only would I be leaving my new friends, but also my grandparents, my cousins, my aunts and uncles (being an only child, my extended family is very important to me), my church, and my youth group; in short, everyone and everything that I had ever known. I cried for days, but it didn't change the fact that we had to move.

I didn't like New York, or my school, but my mom helped me get through it by telling me to think of it as only temporary. We didn't plan to stay there forever, and as soon as my dad could move on to another job, we would try to move back to Kansas City. About a year later, Dad came home one day and told us he had another job offer ... but it wasn't in Kansas City. This time we would be moving to Boston.

I was disappointed, but in learning to cope with these two major moves in just as many years, I had to grow up very quickly (not that I'm there yet!). The most important thing I've learned is that no matter where I go, God is always right there beside me. I've learned to depend on Him when the going gets rough, and the last few years have been pretty rough. But God is working everything out just like He promised He would. And you know what else I've discovered? Life continues, regardless of where I live. I can choose either to join in or to retreat. The choice is mine. And this time I've decided to join in, to live in the here and now, not in my yesterdays or my tomorrows.

Ashley Freeman
Age 17

Notice that the stiffest tree is most easily cracked, while the bamboo or willow survives by bending with the wind.

Bruce Lee

When You Know You're Going to Hate the Change

As I changed into my pajamas, I took in all the things around me. This would be one of the last nights that I would spend in "my house." My house, with its five acres of beautiful country land, three dogs, three cats, and an old railroad track where I often went to talk with God, or to just get away. I remembered the times I'd had friends over to spend the night and we'd played hide-and-go-seek late into the night; and how my best friend, Emily, and I had stayed up until one in the morning once, talking, singing, and laughing.

Now, all that would be only a memory. This would be one of the last nights I would spend in my room, but just as I was lost in reflection, I heard a knock on my door.

"You ready to make brownies?" Emily said.

"Sure, hold on," I answered. "I'll be there in a sec."

Emily and I always made brownies. I figured we were doing it "for old times' sake," since now that I was moving to a horrid place called Vero Beach, our brownie-making days would soon be over.

Vero Beach, or "Zero" Beach as I'd come to call it, was going to ruin my life. I just knew it. Everyone there seemed so happy, so thrilled to be living there. They didn't know the pain I was going through, trying to cope with moving and leaving all my best friends in the world. So I was angry with them. I was also angry with my parents for wanting to move there. I was angry with everyone and everything for the stupidest reasons in the world, but at the time that's all that mattered to me.

Emily and I quickly made a batch of brownies, consumed them, and started to get ready for bed. As I was reading my Bible, I noticed that Emily was curled up with a towel over her head (she always has something over her head when she's asleep). But this night it was different.

Worried, I asked, "What's wrong?"

"I don't want you to move away!" she said, the tears streaming down her face. That was the beginning of "Crying Fest '99." We sobbed and wept all night.

It's amazing how many tears we shed over my move to Vero. But now that I'm here, it doesn't feel like "Zero Beach" anymore. It feels like the place where God wanted me all along. I believe some of the people I've met here really needed me in their life right now, or rather, needed God. And I've been able to share Christ's love with them. To me, Vero Beach was sort of like that mystery soup that your mom makes. You convince yourself that it's going to be disgusting, but once you get a taste of it, you discover that you not only like it, you love it!

Samantha Morgan
Age 13

Don't fear change—embrace it.

Anthony J. D'Angelo

A Step Toward Healing

If you've recently moved to new surroundings, make a list of five things you can do to discover more about your new location.

Even if they're not easy to see, find three positive aspects of your move, then call or write an old friend and share them with him or her.

Chapter 4

Saying Goodbye to a Grandparent

Blessed are those who mourn, for they will be comforted.
                                                    MATTHEW 5:4

Grandparents are special people. They've lived a lot of life, and because of that, they usually have their priorities in order. They know people are more important than jobs, houses, cars, or money. Experience has been their teacher, and they're eager to impart all the life lessons they've learned to anyone who'll listen. Unconditional love comes much easier for grandparents, too. Your behavior has little to do with their love for you. They want the best for you, of course, and from you, but they love you no matter what. They also seem to take life in stride, knowing that if things don't go right today, there's always tomorrow. They've seen a lot of tomorrows in their lifetimes, and they'd be the first to tell you that no matter how hopeless a situation looks today, another tomorrow is just around the corner, so don't ever give up. Grandparents tell it like it is on other issues, too. They realize their time on this earth is limited, so they don't waste it mincing words.

Both of my paternal grandparents died before I got to know them, but I do have memories of my maternal grandparents. My grandfather was tall and lean, and he used to walk me through the field behind his house and pick flowers and berries for me. I'd usually eat enough berries to dye my lips and a good portion of my cheeks and hands bright red.

My grandmother lived longer than my grandfather, so I have more memories of her. I even spent a summer with her in Arkansas when I was fourteen years old, and later she came to live with us for awhile in California.

My fondest memory of my grandmother had to do with my boyfriend (now husband), Russ. Like Grandpa, Russ demonstrated his love by giving me flowers. Every month he'd send roses on the anniversary of our first date. For our first-month anniversary, he sent one rose. For our second, he sent two. And so on. The roses would usually arrive while I was at high school. My grandmother would mark the date on her calendar, then stand by the window watching for the florist's truck to pull up in front of our house.

Grandmother got to accept most of the deliveries, but she died before Russ and I married (we were up to forty-two roses by then). Even though she had been blessed with a long and healthy life, it was still difficult to say goodbye.

If you've recently lost a grandparent, you may be wondering how you're going to make it without his or her unconditional love, exuberant enthusiasm over your achievements, and well of wisdom that has always been available to you. Yet, you will. The support and love of your grandparent will remain in your heart long after your loss, and you'll find comfort in the knowledge that your life is so much richer because your grandparents were a part of it.

When the Clouds Part

I think the hardest death I've had to face was that of my grandfather. Toward the end of his life, I could always find Grandpa in his big, blue easy chair with his oxygen on one side and his remote on the other. He couldn't speak much anymore, but he could still listen. Grandma said we were so much alike. We loved the same foods and had the same opinions. I remember one afternoon before he died, I was short on money for college books. When I got to his house, he asked me to read him the Twenty-third Psalm. When I opened the Bible I found $500, just enough for my books and some lunch. Grandpa loved the Twenty-third Psalm, and reading the passage for him that day gave me hope. It told me he wasn't afraid to die, and even more it said that he was ready to go. It was a constant effort for Grandpa to get even one breath, so how could I ask him to stay and suffer for me?

When he called me into his hospital room one week before he died, he told me three things: one—never to smoke, two—how much he loved me, and three—that he believed in me and my dreams. I will always carry that conversation with me.

I was at work that cloudy day when the call came in for me to get to the hospital "as quickly as possible." I got into the little T-1000 which Grandpa had bought me and raced to the hospital. On the way I noticed a cloud giving way to the sun, and I knew at that moment that Grandpa had gone to be with Jesus. I said my goodbyes in my car. When I arrived at the hospital, I learned that my grandpa had already passed. Later, I discovered that the time of his death was the exact moment that the cloud gave way. The Son shone His light into my grieving soul that day and gave me peace and the comfort of knowing Grandpa was safe and I would one day be with him again.

Anonymous

Be still and know that I am God.

PSALM 46:10

When You Least Expect It

My grandmother died in August 1999. She needed surgery for a heart valve replacement, but we were told it was "routine." My aunts, uncle, and cousins were there, and we all got to see her right before they wheeled her into the operating room. Her last words to us were, "Just love each other. Promise me that you'll love each other."

We didn't realize it at the time, but those were the last words we'd ever hear her say.

The surgery initially went fine, but when the medical staff tried to take her off the heart-lung machine, things took a turn for the worse. Despite all their efforts, they couldn't get her heart to pump again on its own. The muscle was too weak. They kept her on the machine all night, and there were a few signs of improvement, but then she started to worsen again. We prayed through the night, but the reality was that it was time for her to go to her eternal home.

This was my first experience with losing a close loved one. As a family, we pulled together and began to sing worship songs in the hospital room. It was a beautiful way to say goodbye, and I'm glad we got to give that to her!

Losing my grandmother was the hardest thing I've had to go through in my fourteen years of life, but with time, and God's strength and grace, things have gotten easier. My faith has strengthened, too. Before her death, I was drifting, not really knowing what I believed, but now, I know that everything is going be OK. God is in control and has a perfect plan! I trust Him and am closer to Him now than I ever was before. And yes, Grandma, we are remembering to "just love each other."

Christina Fernandez
15 years old

Precious in the sight of the Lord is the death of his saints.

PSALM 116:15

When Your Grandpa Is "Broken"

There was a time in my life when I thought that God was punishing me for some awful sin that I had committed. I thought that because I was a sinner, God had given me a grandpa who wasn't like other grandpas. I thought God had given me a "broken grandpa."

When my grandfather was forty-three, he was diagnosed with Parkinson's Disease. This is a debilitating disease where my grandfather's body won't do what his brain tells it to do. The disease affects all of his muscles. Right now, his "smiler" is temporarily out of order, and talking to him is a difficult task because he can't verbalize very well. Even though deep down inside I know he would love to play a game of catch or go on a bike ride with his grandkids, he physically can't.

Under what doctors call the "Parkinson's Mask," my grandpa is an amazing man. He lives on the land he loves near a small town in Minnesota. He farmed this land his entire life, but now he's content to watch his only son farm it. Even in the midst of his trials, my grandpa counts his blessings. He knows that God has a plan for everything in life, even our trials.

Now that I'm older, I am beginning to see God's hand in it all, too. God wasn't punishing me, nor did he give me a "broken" grandpa. He gave me a role model, a perfect grandpa from whom I can learn so much. God is using my grandpa's strong faith to teach me, to teach all of us, that despite the tough times we go through, and the hardships that seem to pop up like weeds, God is always with us. Death may be imminent, but with every breath we take, we must continue to look up, and we must never miss an opportunity to count our blessings.

I know the day is coming when I'll have to say goodbye to Marlin Vis, my "perfect" grandfather, but I take comfort in knowing that he'll be waiting for me there in heaven, smiling like he used to before Parkinson's stole his smile, and ready and able to finally play catch.

Ashley Vanden Bosch
Age 13

When the heart grieves over what it has lost, the spirit rejoices over what it has left.

Sufi epigram

Now that you are gone,
my heart accepts it as just
a change of address.

Haiku by Diantha Ain

A Step Toward Healing

If you had to sum up your grandmother or grandfather's personality in one word, what would it be?

Write down a favorite story that your grandmother or grandfather once told you.

Chapter 5

Saying Goodbye to Limitations

I can do everything through him who gives me strength.
PHILIPPIANS 4:13

Limitations. We all have them in some form or fashion. Yet most of us don't allow our limitations to define what we can or cannot do. We take our limitations as a challenge to see how far beyond them we can go. In fact, people who seem to accomplish the least in life aren't those with nature-imposed limitations, but those with self-imposed ones. Self-imposed limitations are far more debilitating than anything nature can give us. People with nature-imposed limitations seem to have a spirit that drives them to not only achieve in spite of their limitations, but soar above them.

Like my sister-in-law, Marie.

Marie and my brother, Lee, were high school sweethearts. After graduating, my brother went on to Bible college, and he and Marie married when they were both twenty-two years old. I remember their wedding well because I was only twelve years old at the time, and it was my very first experience with wearing high heels. I didn't like it very much. I'm more the sneaker type. I didn't like trying to balance myself in those heels and having to sit through the entire reception in them, as well as wearing that fancy dress, which was just killing me.

And then, of course, there was my hair. Whose idea were those little pin curls lacquered to my forehead anyway? And shall I mention the pillbox hat with the netting that fell down just below my eyes? Definitely not me. Yet everyone there felt compelled to pinch my cheek and tell me how "lovely" I looked.

The one who really did look lovely was the bride. And my brother looked pretty good himself. It was a beautiful, romantic wedding, and soon they were off on their honeymoon and headed for a blessed life together.

Marie was a special girl. She had developed rheumatic fever when she was a young child, and it had damaged her heart. She had to take daily medications, and was told she should never have children.

About a year after their marriage, she was told something else. Marie was told she needed open-heart surgery. Without it, she had no more than two years to live.

Yet the surgery was risky. The doctors gave her only a 50-50 chance of surviving it. I can't imagine being twenty-three years old and having to make that kind of a decision. Marie and my brother prayed about it, and she decided to pass on the risky surgery and enjoy however much time she had left. They prayed for God to heal her, if it was in His will, and sincerely believed that He would.

About a year after receiving the devastating news, while ministering at a church in Albany, New York, my sister-in-law suffered a heart attack and passed away. She was twenty-four years old.

It was on my fourteenth birthday.

To this day, I don't know why Marie had to die at such a young age and leave such a beautiful marriage. It didn't seem fair. She was gentle and kind, and loved by all who knew her. What possible good could come out of such a tragedy?

Yet, some good did come out of it. It wasn't until a decade later, when my own son was born with congenital heart disease. My husband and I were given the same choice—open-heart surgery to repair the hole in his heart or the risk of a shortened life span. Because of Marie we had the courage we needed to make that difficult decision. We chose the surgery, which, thanks to advanced medical technology, had improved so much over the years that his chances for survival were far greater. Our son had two heart surgeries, and today, he's twenty-four years of age and is doing beautifully.

And who knows how many other lives were touched by Marie's love, her life, and her testimony? Marie was a special girl. She certainly had physical limitations, but she didn't let them slow her down from serving God, loving life, and living every minute of it to the fullest.

Limitations? Marie didn't waste a second of her life looking at them. Neither should we.

When the Blessings Outweigh the Struggles

The difference between stumbling blocks and stepping-stones is how you use them.

Source unknown

Dana was my eldest sibling. She was born on January 20, 1980, with cerebral palsy and was unable to eat or drink on her own, speak, or even control her physical movements. From the time she was very young, she lived in a residential-style hospital in Columbus, Ohio. Dana came home every other weekend, and we could visit her at the hospital whenever we wanted.

Even though I wouldn't get much of a response from her, I loved playing with Dana. I have pictures of me just laying with her, or playing Gameboy while sitting close enough for her to see. I remember special occasions like Christmas morning. My parents would carry Dana to a beanbag chair and we would all open gifts. Just having her there with us was awesome.

I knew Dana had a life-altering disease, but I didn't fully understand the gravity of it. One day she became ill, and her body was just too weak to fight anymore. I had been staying at my grandparents' house and was outside roller-skating when my parents and grandparents came home and told me what had happened. I remember my dad saying to me, "Your sister went and saw Jesus today...." At nine years of age, I couldn't fully understand the concept of death, but I knew I had lost the only sister I would ever have.

To this day, my memories of Dana are vivid. I remember her laugh. I remember how she moved. And I remember how beautiful she was. The most wonderful image I have of Dana, though, is that of a girl who could never walk, talk, or eat on her own, now running alongside God in heaven. Not only is she running, but she's singing. Singing with a voice so amazing, I can't even imagine it with my limited earthly mind. It's the image of a girl who no longer knows pain or discomfort. A girl with a perfect body, in a perfect place. That's my sister, Dana.

Kelly Woodruff
Age 18

When Others Want to Help

"Can you manage that, honey?"

I smile at the lady behind the counter and mentally remind myself that she's only trying to be helpful, but the comment still rankles. Can I manage that? It's a stupid cup of coffee. Instead, I toss out a "Got it, thanks," as I collect my purse, crutches, and a bag of doughnuts along with the coffee and maneuver to the door, more than aware that several pairs of eyes are watching my departure with a mixture of fascination and curiosity.

Can I manage? What a question. Better than simply "manage," by the grace of God I've learned to thrive since losing my left leg to bone cancer when I was ten years old. A somewhat warped sense of humor and a fierce drive to be independent have helped me navigate through a two-footed society. I was also blessed with parents who encouraged and assisted me in my journey, as well as sisters who loved me enough not to let me get away with anything. But "managing" was never a conscious decision. Neither was thriving. It's just something that happens when you live the life you've been given with all the enthusiasm you can. There's no joy to be found in self-pity, but horseback riding? Now you're talking joy, way-down-deep-inside-to-the-bottom-of-your-soul giddiness!

Following my initial surgery for cancer, I spent two years in a leg brace, watching my friends have all the fun. I couldn't do much, and I quickly grew tired of sitting on the sidelines! Finally, my doctor told my parents he believed amputation was the only option to restore mobility and allow me to live life more normally.

I cried the night my parents told me about that conversation with the doctor. I cried, but not for long. Somehow I knew a whole life awaited me on the other side of the surgeon's knife, a life that included bike riding, roller-skating, tree climbing, and yes, even my beloved horses.

Though I didn't realize it at the time, I now see what a huge role my parents played in my recovery and success as an amputee. Though Mom was with me nearly every moment of my hospital stays, she never coddled me after I returned home. If it was my turn to do the dishes, she made sure I did them. If I deserved a spanking, you can believe she made sure I got one. She treated me like any other ten-year-old, and she even went a step further. She let me fly.

Often, I'd come home with tales of "Guess what I did today?" Mom would listen as I recounted my latest exploits of climbing trees or swinging from the monkey bars at school, never once letting on that she was cringing inside. In fact, two weeks after the amputation, we took a family trip to the Statue of Liberty and Mom held my crutches so I could navigate to the top of the winding staircase that was too narrow for crutches.

Yes, Mom let me fly, but it was Daddy who built my wings. My father would lie awake at night figuring out ways to make my prosthesis more adaptable to my activities. When I wanted to be a cheerleader, he replaced the leather strap that held the prosthesis around my waist with a bungee cord that would stretch and allow me to do splits. Dad was also the one who came up with the idea of a stationary bike pedal on the three-wheeler I rode until I gained my balance enough to resume riding my two-wheeled bike. And as I grew, it was my father who figured out that he could remove the foot part of the prosthesis and add extensions from the bottom, to accommodate my growth.

There's another person who's responsible for my joyous flight through life. When I was fifteen years old, I met and began dating John. We ended up getting married shortly after I turned twenty. How did I know he was the one? For me, it was clear. My prosthesis had two different feet, one for heels and another one for sneakers. John would help me "change" feet after church, and his favorite trick was putting the foot on so that it faced backward when I stood up. Over the years, John has watched me carry both of our children around like a football while on crutches without the least trepidation, perfectly confident that I could more than "manage," though he will still occasionally tease me with the remark that he married me for my handicapped parking placard. John knows if I need help, I'll ask. And every once in awhile, I will ... just to make him feel needed.

Learning to accept assistance with grace has been a struggle for me, but I'm finally coming to realize that most people offer aid out of love or genuine concern, not pity. And as much as I hate to admit it, sometimes I really do need their help.

Still, I'm convinced that living my life focused on enjoying what I have, instead of mourning what I've lost, has brought me more joy than self-pity ever would have brought. Only my leg is gone. I'm still here. Yes, I can manage.

Chris Redner

Argue for your limitations, and sure enough they're yours.

Richard Bach

You gain strength, courage, and confidence by every experience in which you really stop to look fear in the face. You must do the thing which you think you cannot do.

Eleanor Roosevelt

A Step Toward Healing

Would you say you spend more of your time seeing your limitations or your possibilities?

Make a list of the things that you feel you can't do, then make another list of the things you can do. How do you feel when you look at your "Can Do" list?

Chapter 6

Saying Goodbye As You Answer God's Call

My presence will go with you, and I will give you rest.

EXODUS 33:14

Following God's will for our lives can take us to some scary places sometimes, can't it? That's because God's will usually requires us to stretch, to go beyond our talents, our understanding, and our comfort zone. Moses had to stretch when God asked him to go and speak to Pharaoh. Public speaking wasn't one of Moses' talents, or at least he didn't think it was, so when God asked him to be the one to deliver his message to Pharaoh, Moses was hesitant. "I'll go," he finally said, "but you've gotta let me take my brother, Aaron, with me."

God asks us to do things beyond our capabilities probably so that when it's accomplished, there won't be any question as to who deserves the credit. If we know beyond a shadow of a doubt that we couldn't do it on our own, we won't be trying to steal the credit from God.

So we're asked to stretch.

If you're being asked to stretch, to leave your comfort zone, to say goodbye to good friends, relatives, and your home life as you know it to follow God's will for your life, take courage. You're in good company.

When Everything Is New

As September 2000 approached, I knew I would be leaving my home in Lagos, Nigeria, to continue my premedical studies and, hopefully, one day fulfill my dream of becoming a missionary doctor. At first, leaving home seemed exciting. New experiences. New friends. A new place to live. But two weeks before I was scheduled to leave, reality started to set in. I was going to be leaving home, not for another state in Nigeria or another country in Africa, but for New Brunswick, Canada. New Brunswick was three flights and fifteen hours away from Lagos. I was leaving everything I knew and going to a place where I knew no one but God. I had so many fears in my heart. Would my friends remember me? Would I lose those precious relationships I had worked so hard to build over the years? What in the world was I doing?

I also knew, though, that God wanted me to go to New Brunswick. I knew that beyond any doubt. So I said goodbye to my friends and family, and with tears in my eyes I was off.

On the flight, I listened to Steven Curtis Chapman's song "In His Eyes" and held my new teddy, Phimmey, so close to me and talked to him so desperately that I'm sure my fellow passengers wondered about my mental stability.

Two weeks after I arrived in New Brunswick, I found myself bringing out the pictures of my friends and crying all over again. It was then that I felt God speak to my heart and say, "I've been through your pain, dear child. I know what it is to miss home and familiar surroundings. I left My Father and My home in heaven to come to earth to die for you. Do you know I got homesick, too? I missed the angels, the streets of gold, and all that I had there. But I also knew I had a purpose. Just like you have a purpose. So don't be afraid. I love you and I'll be right by your side with every new step you take."

A whole school year has gone by since that night, and you know what? God has been faithful. I've met new friends, found a new home church, and even gotten used to the freezing weather and new surroundings. And thanks to the Internet, I'm still able to keep in touch with my family and friends back in Nigeria. Now, whenever I get homesick, I just remember that I'm not going through anything that Jesus himself didn't go through. Like Hebrews 4:15-16 says, "This High priest of ours understands our weaknesses since He had the same temptations we do, though He never once gave way to them and sinned. So let us come boldly to the throne of God and stay there to receive His mercy and find grace to help us in our times of need."

Opeyemi Atilola
Age 19

Each experience
blends texture and strength into
the fabric of life.

Haiku by Diantha Ain

When You Choose to Lose and Gain So Much

I experienced one of my greatest losses last year when my family and I moved to Romania to become long-term missionaries. I was fifteen at the time and, up to that point, I had lived what you might call an ordinary life. Before making this monumental decision, we had spent plenty of time in prayer, and had received wise counsel from our pastor and other missionaries.

Usually we don't choose to lose. Most loss comes unexpectedly or against our will. But in my case, it was different. I wanted to go to the mission field because, like my mother and father, I knew it was God's will for our lives.

But then the losses began. We put our house up for sale and started packing. You never realize how attached you are to things until you have to start doing without them. I felt an overwhelming sadness as I looked for the last time at the little knick-knacks and memories I had collected over the years—stuffed animals, class portraits, figurines. We sold or gave away much of our furniture, and as our house became emptier and emptier, my sense of belonging started to unravel. The beds, the sofa, the dining room table, the piano, and even the old, worn welcome mat—everything went. In their places were left huge, gaping spaces where only the bare walls stared back at us. Near the end, it didn't even seem like our house anymore. It had become a strange, cold, eerie place. We had lived in that house for thirteen years, and I knew that, once we left, there would be no returning.

There were also our pets to be dealt with. My brother and I love animals, so we always had plenty of them. Through the years our house had seen hamsters, mice, frogs, rabbits, cats, dogs, a myriad of fish, and even hermit crabs. Most of these were fairly easy to give away or release, but it was hard to part with our beloved dog, who had been my faithful friend for the last six years.

Still, losing the house, our pets, and all our "stuff" couldn't compare with the pain of leaving the people who had become so dear to us, especially our church family.

I began to wonder if there was anything left to lose. Yet God is faithful, and He continued to give us peace—the kind of peace that surpasses understanding. Peace that comes only from doing what God has called you to do.

In late July 2000, we arrived in Romania, almost exactly a year after we had first prayed as a family about becoming missionaries. I'd like to say that the loss stopped at that point, but unfortunately, it continues. Just yesterday I received an e-mail saying that a boy from my youth group had died. I knew him well, and the news hit me hard. How I wish right now that I could be there at his funeral with the other teens who knew him.

Yet, just as the loss continues, so does the gain. Since we have come to Romania, we've had the awesome privilege to share Christ with many people, and to make new friends. Yes, we get discouraged sometimes and wonder if the people with whom we work are ever going to change, but then we remember that our job is only to plant the seeds and leave the rest to God.

Saying goodbye to my will and yes to God's was the best thing I've ever done. Being a missionary isn't easy; there's no way to overlook that. But it is also one of the most rewarding and fulfilling things for a Christian to do. We're all commanded to spread the Good News, but I realize not everyone is called by God to go to a foreign country. That was our calling. If it's yours, follow it and don't look at the loss. If you happen to have a different calling on your life, follow that. But as you do, remember to pray for the missionaries around the world, and if you can, keep in touch with a few of them. It means more than you'll ever know.

Christina Marian
Age 16

I can do everything through him who gives me strength.

PHILIPPIANS 4:13

When You're Always Saying Goodbye

I never liked saying goodbye. I wasn't good at it at all. But suddenly I found myself saying it a lot—almost every weekend, in fact.

It started two years ago when my sister, Kelly, and I began traveling, touring the country as gospel singers. Every week we would have to tell our family and friends goodbye. At the beginning, they were tearful goodbyes. But after awhile, our departures became more routine and there were no more tears.

While on the road, though, we've met some wonderful people. Many have become our lifelong friends. We've shared stories about our families and our ministries and about how God is working in our lives.

We've also made many good friends among the people we've met at the various concerts or churches where we've ministered. Sometimes you can meet someone and feel like you've known that person all your life.

Yet just like at home, there are goodbyes to be said on the road, too. We're never in one city very long before we have to move on to our next destination.

Sometimes I miss the stability of being in the same place and seeing the same people. But I wouldn't trade the friendships I've made over these last few years for anything. And anyway, saying goodbye now just makes saying hello again someday that much sweeter.

Annie McRae
The McRaes

What is more, I consider everything a loss compared to the surpassing greatness of knowing Christ Jesus my Lord, for whose sake I have lost all things. I consider them rubbish, that I may gain Christ.

PHILIPPIANS 3:8

Blazing a new trail
presents an awesome challenge
that brave hearts accept.

Haiku by Diantha Ain

A Step Toward Healing

Have you prayed for God to show you His plan for your life?

Why do you think it's important to trust God and follow His plan for our lives?

Chapter 7

Saying Goodbye to a Parent

My soul is weary with sorrow; strengthen me according
to your word.

PSALM 119:28

When my mother died, I wanted to curl up in a corner and just
be alone. I wanted to run. I wanted to slam my fist onto the
table right there in the Intensive Care waiting room. I wanted
to do something. Anything that would release the pain and frus-
tration I was feeling. But all I could do was cry. I had held it all
in for eight months while we were fighting the lymphoma.
During each chemotherapy treatment or blood transfusion, I
had tried to be a cheerleader for Mom, convincing her that she
was going to beat the cancer. Now it was painfully obvious that
I had been wrong.

Good people aren't supposed to die. At least that's what we
tell ourselves, isn't it? Kind, loving, generous people like my
mother should get to live a long and healthy life. If some people
have to leave this world early, why shouldn't it be the mean,
grumpy ones? They're not having a good time anyway. Why do
people who are making a difference in this world, making it a
better place by their presence, have to leave before we're ready

to let them go? It doesn't make a lot of sense, does it? It didn't make sense for me, either, that night in the hospital when I heard the Code Blue over the PA announcing that my mother's journey from this life to the next had begun.

So I had questions. Lots of questions. Do you know it's OK to ask God questions? When we don't understand why something has happened, it's all right to talk things over with Him. We might not get an answer right away, and we might not find out the reason for certain circumstances in our lives until we're face to face with God Himself, but what God can and will give us now is a peace. A peace in knowing that He's in control of the situation and He loves us very, very much. It may not feel like love when we're saying that reluctant goodbye, but God understands how difficult it is to have to stand by and watch a loved one pass through death. He knows the hurt we feel. And He also knows that the pain would be lessened if only we could see the same big picture He sees. From His vantage point, He can clearly see beyond our tears to a heavenly reunion celebration that's only "moments" away. He wants us to capture that vision, too.

When an Ordinary Day Becomes a Day You'll Never Forget

October 10, 1995. Tuesday morning. Not a dreary Monday or a happy Friday; just plain old Tuesday. The buzz of my alarm clock jolted me awake. I stumbled across the hall carpet and stepped onto the cold tile floor of the bathroom. It was the kind of cold that causes your feet to cramp, shocking you into reality.

I had just flipped on the light and pried open my eyes to slip in my contacts and begin my normal morning routine when my father knocked on my door and said, "Jeni, I need your help! I think your mom is dying!"

I don't know why, but I just assumed Mom was having some minor trouble with her heart again and that Dad was overreacting. Mom had just received a good bill of health from her doctor, but I knew Dad would probably rush her to the hospital in a panic, and I would end up watching my little brother at home. It was the routine. Then Mom, of course, would refuse to let the doctors poke around on her and would eventually convince them to let her go back home. I'd get to bed late and would have to miss school again and.... Another knock on the door stopped my train of thought.

"Jeni! I don't think she's breathing." Dad's voice sounded frightened. I knew this time that the emergency was real.

I walked out of the bathroom and into the hall. I saw my dad hand my little brother the telephone and tell him to go stand at the end of the driveway and wait for an ambulance. When I turned and walked back into my parents' room, I felt as though I was no longer in my body. I was simply a stranger viewing this tragic scene as it unfolded. My mother was lying on the bed, motionless, pale, and empty. Her auburn hair seemed dull against the faded blue comforter. Even the butterflies on the translucent curtain hung dismally in the air.

As I walked to her bedside, the skills I had learned in my CPR class came back to me with God-sent clarity. I checked her breathing and pulse. Nothing. I instructed my dad to clear the floor, and I moved her there. She didn't seem heavy at all. Her body was light, like all the burdens of the world had been lifted from her. I began CPR, and my father quickly caught on and helped. At one point I looked at my dad with tears in my eyes and said, "It's too late, Dad. She's gone."

It seemed like hours before the paramedics came into her room and took over the life-saving measures. I wanted them to use some miracle drug or say a special prayer that would turn the situation around and bring my mother back, but with each passing second, her life seemed to slip further and further away.

I ran into my room, shut the door behind me, and called my youth pastor to tell him what had happened. His wife assured me she would be there as soon as possible.

When I came out of my room and heard the EMT ask my dad which funeral home he would prefer they call, my heart sank. I didn't know what to do. I was sixteen years old, and my best friend, my mom, my counselor, my mentor, the woman who had introduced me to Jesus, my lifeline, had just died. Suddenly, everything in my life was different.

They covered my mother with a special pink quilt that had been in our family for years, then we all left her room and shut the door. Friends and family quickly made their way to the house and waited for the funeral home to come. Unnoticed, I quietly walked back into her room and locked the door behind me. I sat down beside my mother and ran my fingers through her auburn hair. I cried out, wept, and said goodbye. It was the most difficult thing I have ever had to do.

For weeks I felt numb, confused, and scared. I was an emotional zombie on the outside, but inside my life was spinning. I questioned why my mother had had to die, and I questioned God. Eventually, I came to realize that in all my pain, God hadn't left me alone. He was there for me all along, and He even sent others to be there for me, too. That day when I called my youth director's wife, I had no idea what kind of friendship would grow from that. She became my surrogate mother.

It wasn't easy, especially during those first few months when the pain was so fresh, but God put her and many other people in my path who loved me beyond my wildest expectations—an aunt who offered me a second home, a surrogate mother who hugged and comforted me, friends who listened and held me as I cried, and a church family that showered me with prayer, praise, and abundant support.

God has used this event in my life in ways that I never would have expected. Because of my loss, I have been able to comfort others who are going through a similar tragedy in their lives. Yes, in the midst of my turmoil, God was there to cradle me in His arms, just as He had promised He would be. It was my mother who first taught me that biblical truth, and through her death, God has proved it to be true.

Jeni Woods
Age 22

Trust in the Lord with all your heart and lean not on your own understanding; in all your ways acknowledge him, and he will make your paths straight.

PROVERBS 3:5-6

When You Know They're in a Better Place

I had to say goodbye to my father when I was ten years of age. After undergoing an operation to remove a brain tumor, he had a stroke and passed away. That was seven years ago, and it still hurts. Some days are better than others. His birthday and Father's Day are especially difficult, and whenever I think about not having my father at my high school graduation, or at my wedding to walk me down the aisle, it's almost more than I can bear.

Yet even in my grief, I know I have much to be thankful for. I'm thankful that I had my father for as long as I did, especially since he almost died after his first surgery, when I was only two years old. But he didn't. The Lord allowed him to live for eight more wonderful years. During that time I was able to get to know my father and gather many wonderful memories to tell my own children someday—like when we used to go fishing or just sit together and talk.

I'm also thankful that I'm even here. My mother tells me that I was a miracle baby because of my father's illness. Yet seventeen years ago, I came into this world happy and healthy. Frankly, I think God gave me to my mother so I would be here to help take care of her after my father's death.

Losing a parent hurts. It hurts a lot. But I take comfort in the fact that I've been given so many blessings, and now that my father is with the Lord, I know that he, too, is healthy and whole again.

Julie Witner
Age 17

If we had no winter, the spring would not be so pleasant; if we did not sometimes taste of adversity, prosperity would not be so welcome.

Anne Bradstreet

The warmth of God's love
lifts my deflated spirit
to euphoric heights.

Haiku by Diantha Ain

When All You Have Are Memories

I was about five years old when my mother was diagnosed with cancer. I was too young then to fully understand what the diagnosis meant. All I knew was that I would go along with her whenever she went for chemotherapy, and I would color in the coloring books in the waiting room.

I also remember that each time my mother was hospitalized, one of my aunts would come over to our house to take care of me and my three older brothers. It was a long drive to the medical center, and our father usually ended up spending the night there with Mom.

I especially remember the last time my mother had to go to the hospital. I had a feeling I wouldn't see her again. I was only nine years old and couldn't understand why she had to go away again. I cried for her to stay, but she told me she couldn't.

My intuition soon proved to be correct. That was the last time I would see my mother. She never came home again.

It's taken me a long time to get over the death of my mother, and I'd be less than honest if I didn't say that growing up without a mom has been difficult at times. There are certain topics that I don't feel comfortable discussing with my dad or my older brothers. Luckily, though, I have lots of aunts to fill in that gap, as well as some of my friends' moms.

I was young when my mother passed away, but I still have plenty of wonderful memories of her. She took such good care of us, even in the midst of her own illness. In fact, just before she died that wintry day, she told my dad to make sure I wore something on my legs at her funeral so I wouldn't get cold. That was my mom—always thinking of her kids. She was a good mom, and no matter how many years pass, I know I'll always be thinking of her, too.

Laura Braun
Age 15

As I kneel to pray,
the love of God enfolds me
like an angel's wings.

Haiku by Diantha Ain

When You Deliver on a Dream

I was three years old when my father joined the State Department. One of the perks of working for the government in that capacity was that we got the wonderful opportunity of traveling overseas. We've lived in Sweden, in Malawi (which is a small country on the continent of Africa), and even in St. Petersburg, Russia.

We didn't stay very long in Russia, though, because six months after we arrived there, my mother began having terrible headaches. The headaches were a symptom of what was later diagnosed as a brain tumor.

We returned to the United States, where my mother had surgery, radiation treatment, and numerous CAT scans. When it appeared she was improving, my father took a job in Washington, D.C., and we began to settle in and make friends in our new home.

Just as life was settling back down to normal, however, everything changed yet again. Near the end of the school year, my mother was diagnosed with another brain tumor. This one was worse than the first and was growing much faster. In spite of all the wonderful care she was receiving, it began to look like there was little chance my mom would survive. She was losing her ability to speak, and at times she would digress to childlike behaviors. It was heartbreaking to watch the stages of the disease. My mother didn't seem like my mother anymore. It was as though I had lost her already.

In August of that year, our worst fears came true. My mother passed away. My mother, who had shared the adventures of so many different countries with me, had made me feel safe and loved, and had led me to Christ in Malawi when I was seven years old, was now gone.

Around three o'clock that morning, I went downstairs to say my final goodbye. When I entered the room, I could feel an unexplainable peace. My mother was no longer there in her body. It was as if Jesus Himself had gently escorted Elisabeth Joy Grover home.

According to her wishes, she was cremated and her remains buried next to a redwood tree. After all our world travel, my mother's dream was to be buried by a stately old American redwood tree. I'm glad we were able to make her dream come true.

Megan Grover
Age 14

But you, O God, do see trouble and grief; you consider it
to take it in hand. The victim commits himself to you;
you are the helper of the fatherless.

PSALM 10:14

A Step Toward Healing

If you've experienced the loss of a parent, what one life lesson
do you believe he or she would have most wanted to leave with
you?

Recall a fond memory of your mother or father and share it with
someone this week.

Chapter 8

When Family Ties Come Undone

When I am afraid, I will trust in you.

PSALM 56:3

I suppose there is such a thing as an amicable divorce, one where everybody gets along—the divorcing couple, the ex-wife with new wife, the new husband with the former husband, the stepchildren with the stepparents, the old mother-in-law with the new mother-in-law, the old dog with the new cat. Yet, that's more the exception than the rule. There are major adjustments that usually have to be made when a family is faced with divorce. Divorce means change. Lots of change. And change is often painful. Or, at the very least, uncomfortable.

As difficult as it is for the man and woman who are divorcing, however, divorce is no doubt hardest on the children. Children often feel they're to blame when their parents split up.

"If only I had been more helpful around the house, Mom and Dad might have stayed together."

"Why did I have to get a 'D' on my report card? If it weren't for me, my parents wouldn't be fighting all the time."

It's easy to put the blame on yourself, especially when you hear your parents fighting night after night, and your report card and chores get brought up right in the middle of the argument.

Now, granted, your mother and father would no doubt love to have you help more around the house, and higher grades on your report card are certainly going to put them in a better mood, but couples don't usually get divorced over a "D" in Science, or a health code violation in your closet. Your parents are dealing with deeper issues, ones that you may not even be aware of.

You need to know, too, that just because your parents are convinced they no longer love each other, doesn't mean that they have any doubts about their love for you. If you're starting to wonder about that, I would suggest you have a talk with your mother and father, either together or with each one privately and let them reassure you personally that your relationship with them is intact.

Ideally, we wish all marriages would work out. Unfortunately, that's not the case. Some very wonderful men and women end up divorcing. You can hope and pray that your parents will work things out, but if they don't, you can survive the impending changes if you hang on to your faith, believe that you're loved, and don't get caught up in the emotional tug of war. Talk to a trusted friend or relative, minister, or counselor to help get you through this transitional period. Even if you're confused and don't know what it is you're feeling, that's OK. It's all right to be confused for awhile. You're going to make it. So will your parents. And even though you didn't create this crisis, you just might come through it stronger, and maybe even determined to work at your own relationships a little harder.

When You Feel Torn in Two

It was another brainstorming session with the teens from our church drama group. Each week, we'd get together, look at the topic for the upcoming teen service, and then talk about how to tackle it through the use of drama. But this week's topic was a greater challenge than usual. It was divorce. The actual topic title given to us was "Divorce Stings." Catchy, huh?

On this particular night, only two teens, Angie and Rob, showed up. But since they were the only two on our team who were from broken homes, I was glad they were there. Their input, I figured, would lend realism to the sketch.

I had no firsthand knowledge of divorce. When I was a teen (back when oversized pants were what the homeless wore and not the latest fashion trend), divorce wasn't as easy or as celebrated. It was rarely the first option considered by a couple, and teens usually downplayed a divorce situation in their home because of a feeling of embarrassment and shame.

Still, we needed a sketch and we were running out of time. To jumpstart our discussion, I approached the chalkboard and wrote down the words "Divorce Stings."

"OK, you guys," I said. "You both know more about this subject than I do, so I really need your help to make our sketch ring true."

Angie cut me off.

"You want it real? How's this? Change the title to 'Divorce Stinks.' Ever since my folks split, there's a part of me I've never been able to get back. For a long time, I felt it was all my fault. I kinda still do," she said. Her words were delivered in a calm and direct manner, far from what I had expected. I quickly captured her words on the board.

"That's good, Ang," I said, excited over the direction of her comments, but overlooking the pain. "I mean, not good in the sense that you feel at fault, but, well, good for the sketch."

It was Rob's turn now. "I hate it when I have to go from one house to the other every other weekend," he said. "Pass The Kid. It's a game without a lot of winners. Sometimes I forget to take the right clothes with me because I'm used to having them in my own room, not my stepbrother's room." He paused, then continued. "And the strange thing is, they expect me to like it."

"Yeah," agreed Angie. "That's the worst. It's like we're, I don't know, furniture or something. This week he gets us, next week she does."

My chalk flew across the board, trying its best to capture their cold pain with each word. Rob chimed in again, "My stepfather is twice as hard on me as my real dad is. He thinks he has to be, I guess, because he's my stepfather. And my own father doesn't think he can discipline me at all anymore or I'll hate him. Crazy. Nothing's the same. My whole world changed overnight. Rules aren't rules anymore. No relationship is secure."

"My parents fought over me in court, and even now they can't seem to agree on anything except how tearing up our family was 'better for us in the long run,'" said Angie. "How could they say that? I don't remember being brought into the discussion. And I sure didn't ask for a stepsister who borrows my CDs and never gives them back."

"It's like parents don't give us kids any thought," said Rob. "We're the ones who get bounced back and forth, but no one bothers to ask us if that's something we'd like to do."

I couldn't believe the honest pain that was pouring forth from both of them. I continued writing, nodding and encouraging their feelings. I also began to realize that this generation, more than any other, is expected to "handle" divorce more easily, because they are seen as adults much earlier in life. They're expected to adjust to a family split quickly and maturely, without the inconvenience and messiness of adolescent insecurities, fear, or angry flare-ups.

When I finished writing, I turned and asked, "So, what lesson do we want teens and adults to take away from this drama?"

Rob and Angie looked at each other, then turned back to me. "That kids have feelings, too," Angie said. "That we aren't property or a potted plant you rent for a weekend to make the house look a little cozier." Angie's voice quivered as she spoke, and Rob's faux maturity couldn't withstand the onslaught of raw emotions. "Why couldn't they just work it out?" he cried.

Suddenly, my sketch didn't seem so important. The real pain of divorce that I wanted to portray on the stage was being performed right there in front of me. No matter how justified it is or how amicable a couple manages to make it, divorce affects everyone involved. And too often the greatest hurt is suffered by those most innocent in the situation—the kids. Kids who often undeservedly carry the blame for years.

I thanked Angie and Rob for their help and tried to assure them that their parents' divorces weren't their fault. I also told them that God loved both their mothers and their fathers and that if they asked Him, He would help ease the pain of the situation. Their parents still might not get back together, but God could help heal their own hurt. They both said that having the chance to talk about the divorce seemed to help, and we closed in a word of prayer.

And the sketch? I gave the two teens the notes and decided

to let them try their hand at writing it. After all, I was just a playwright writing a script for the stage. Angie and Rob had both already lived it.

Dave Tippett
Playwright

I can't change the direction of the wind, but I can adjust my sails to always reach my destination.

Jimmy Dean

When You Get What You Wish For

I wanted my parents to get divorced. Or so I thought. Their fighting made me so uncomfortable and angry at times that I would yell, "Why don't you just get divorced?!" Yet, I never thought it would actually happen and that years later I would feel guilty for those words.

The year my mother was planning to announce her intentions to leave my father, seven people in our family and our extended family died. First, it was lung cancer, then a brain aneurysm, then emphysema, murder, and a tragic car accident. Until that year I had never known anyone who had died (except an old neighbor lady I didn't really know). Needless to say, I lived most of that year numb.

So my mother held her news one more year. The night she called me to tell me she had filed for divorce from my father, I broke down and sobbed. I had so many emotions—guilt because I knew I had wanted it, fear of what this would mean for our family, sadness because the two people I loved the most in the world no longer loved each other, and confusion.

Because my parents had lived separate lives for years, I tried to tell myself, "How much could really change?" I convinced myself the only difference would be location, and everything else would remain the same. I was wrong. Everything changed! Our house, once the hub, the gathering place for all holidays and special occasions, became empty. Even our extended family seemed to separate. People took sides. My parents wouldn't speak to each other. My brothers were fighting. And as the first-born, I thought it was my job to fix it.

To make matters worse, my father sold our family home and got remarried. When Dad sold the house, he not only sold the only home I'd ever known, he sold it with many of our things still inside. Emotionally, he could not deal with taking down pictures or selling furniture, so he just left them there. (The part that I find amazing is that the new homeowners actually wanted our old stuff, and as far as I know our pictures are still hanging in their rooms!) So there I was—not only had I lost my family as I knew it, but my home and my things as well. I felt misplaced. Like I belonged nowhere. I was unwillingly forced to make a new home, on my own.

It has been five years since the divorce. My parents still don't speak to each other. My youngest brother is still struggling. My other brother married my best friend and they have a family of their own. My father seems to gravitate toward cultivating the relationships in his new family. My mother threw herself into her schooling and work. And I never "fixed" anything.

Despite all this, somehow things are slowly getting better. I am at a new place. No, I don't have a house. I live in an apartment in New York City. My "new place" is a mental, emotional, and spiritual place. My home is in my heart. And no matter how slowly our broken family is healing, my heavenly Father is constant. He promises to never leave nor forsake me. He won't divorce me or sell the home He's preparing for me. When my world changes, His love doesn't change with it. It can be trusted, it will sustain me, and best of all, it's everlasting.

Anonymous

Pain is inevitable; suffering is optional.

M. Kathleen Casey

A Step Toward Healing

If your parents are going through a divorce right now, hopefully they're either receiving, or have already received, marital counseling. Is there a minister, youth pastor, teacher, or trusted friend with whom you can talk and share your feelings?

Even if the divorce means you'll be moving away from your familiar surroundings, think of some ways in which you can keep your daily life as routine as possible during this transitional period.

Chapter 9

Saying Goodbye Too Soon

He tends his flock like a shepherd: He gathers the lambs in his arms and carries them close to his heart; he gently leads those that have young.

ISAIAH 40:11

It's difficult to understand why God would choose to bring babies or young children home before they have had a chance to fully live their lives, isn't it? But without answers, all we can do is trust Him to bring something good out of the pain, disappointment, and loss.

I was nineteen years old, had been married for more than a year, and had already suffered one miscarriage when we learned I was pregnant again. Needless to say, I was excited but apprehensive. The miscarriage had been difficult emotionally. I had been twelve weeks along when I began experiencing severe back pain one night. By morning, I had lost the baby.

Still, everything seemed to be going well with this second pregnancy. I made it beyond the first three months of pregnancy, then four months, and eventually I found myself one week from my due date.

During a routine exam, however, my obstetrician couldn't pick up a heartbeat. He told me not to worry about it, then said he had an overseas trip planned but if labor hadn't started on its own by his return the following week, he would then induce it.

Not worrying about it was easier said than done. The sudden stillness of the life inside me was a constant reminder that something could be seriously wrong. I telephoned our family doctor to discuss the situation, and he was adamant that the baby should be induced as soon as possible.

The following morning I was admitted to the hospital, and some seventeen hours later, I delivered a ten-pound, two-ounce stillborn baby boy.

There's probably no way to describe the sadness and overwhelming feeling of disappointment that follows the death of a baby. I had been given three baby showers. We had bought baby furniture and room decorations. There had been such hope, such excitement and anticipation.

Now, I was making burial arrangements.

My grief and disappointment were only compounded by what took place in the days that followed. A photographer came into my hospital room and asked if I wanted to have a picture taken of my baby. Nurses walked me to the shower, right past the window behind which all the healthy babies were thriving and crying. Several times a day an announcement came over the loudspeaker asking visitors to leave because the babies were being brought to their mothers.

When I returned home, things didn't get much easier. I kept the door to the nursery closed so I wouldn't have to see the crib, but there were still baby magazines, baby product brochures, and hospital bills that arrived in the mail almost daily. Then there were the friends and neighbors who hadn't heard about the loss yet. "Was it a boy or a girl?" they would inquire, excitedly, after glancing down at my newly flattened stomach.

This was a very difficult time in my life, but I did get through it. It was painful, but I did survive. To this day I don't know all the reasons why God would have allowed such a tragedy in our lives, but I can honestly say that good has come from it. And God has blessed us more than I could ever imagine. We have since adopted two sons, and I gave birth to a third son—all within a two-year period of time.

I never got to hold the son we lost, but I know I will one day. And when I do, I won't ever have to say goodbye to him again.

When You Learn an Important Life Lesson

When I was in second grade, I tried to make friends with everyone. I got to go to a school within a school for gifted kids, and our class had first-, second-, and third-graders.

There was this one particularly nice first-grade boy named Denny. I remember him, because we were partners in science together. He was a small, skinny boy, with glasses, freckles, and curly hair. We got along well. Then one day, we heard Denny was leaving our school. We weren't sure why he was leaving, but we all said goodbye to him, then left school for the weekend.

That weekend, Denny died. He had been skating at the roller-skating rink, and collapsed. To this day, no one really knows for certain what happened, but I believe he had an undiagnosed heart condition.

When my mother told me about Denny's death, I cried. I wasn't one of his close friends, but he was still someone I considered a friend. He was just a little kid, barely seven years old.

When we got to school, the guidance counselor was there. At least I had already been informed of the news and was prepared. Many of my classmates heard it for the first time that day.

I remember making cards for his two best friends, Alex and Sam. Somehow doing that seemed to make me feel better. There's something about reaching out to someone else in the midst of your own grief that helps ease the pain a bit.

Also, I didn't fully realize it then, but I learned a life lesson that day back in the second grade, a lesson that would stay with me for as long as I live. Life isn't forever, and we should make the most of it while we're here. I'm trying to do that by living my life to the fullest and keeping my priorities in the proper order.

To this day I miss Denny and think of him, but I know we'll have all eternity to catch up on our memories.

Sara Kelm

No winter lasts forever; no spring skips its turn.

Hal Borland

When You Never Got to Hold Her

When I was seven years old, my mother became pregnant. I was thrilled that there would soon be a new child in the house, and it was even more exciting when I found out the baby was going to be a girl. I already had a four-year-old brother, and I had been wanting a baby sister for years. It was such a dream come true that I didn't even mind sharing my room with her. In fact, I couldn't wait to clear out half the room just to make space for all the baby things we were starting to gather.

The pregnancy was going fine. My mom went to her doctor for her regular appointment and was told that she should expect to give birth to a healthy baby girl at the end of August. That was still a month and a half away. Two days later, though, Mom started into labor. My father was at work, so my mother called my aunt to take her to the hospital.

I don't remember much about the rest of that morning. I recall sitting in the waiting room of the hospital with my brother and two cousins for what seemed like forever, but in reality was about three or four hours. All sorts of possible scenarios ran through my head. At eight years old, my two favorite television shows were *ER* and *Rescue 911*, so I knew a lot of medical terms that most kids my age might not have known, including the risks involved when a baby is born a month and a half prematurely.

Finally, my aunt came into the waiting room to get me and take me to Mom's room. When I entered the room, my mother said softly, "Angela, you aren't going to have a baby sister after all."

"What do you mean?" I asked, a little disappointed, figuring my dreams of a baby girl were dashed with the birth of a new baby brother.

"I've got a baby brother instead?" I asked.

"No, you have a sister," she said, "but she's dead."

My mom and dad proceeded to explain to me that my sister, April, had been stillborn.

I had an overwhelming sense of disappointment that I would never get to meet the sister I had longed for since I was two years old. I didn't quite know how to handle it. There aren't any rule books for how we're supposed to handle life's difficult places. We just do the best we can.

My life changed that summer, and by the time I went back to school in the fall, I was a completely different girl, one pulled so far into a protective shell that she could hardly be reached. I could barely talk to any of the kids at school, and I would cry at the mere mention of babies.

Grieving takes time. We all handle it in our own way, but for even the strongest among us, it takes time. For me, it took two years to get my life back together, to get myself back to the way I had been before my sister died.

Now, nearly six years later, the wound has healed. The scar of the loss is still there, but it doesn't hurt like it did. I still carry a picture of my sister that a wonderful nurse at the hospital took for me that day. And when I do a project on families at school, I always include my sister as part of my family, even though many of the other students don't understand. I realize that no one can fully understand what this kind of loss is like unless they've been through it. I know it's helped me to be more sensitive to those who have experienced a similar loss.

I will always love my sister. And even though there are some people who might say that because April died before birth, she never really existed, I know April Christina Metcalf existed. She may not have gotten to enjoy a life here on this earth with us, but she is a part of our family. She will live forever, both in heaven and in my heart.

Angela Metcalf
Age 14

The soul would have no rainbow had the eyes no tears.

John Vance Cheney

A Step Toward Healing

If you've had to say goodbye to a young child or infant, think of something you can do that will help preserve his or her memory.

The Bible clearly states that little children are precious to God. Can you find comfort in knowing that your loved one is resting in His arms even now?

Chapter 10

Being There

A friend loves at all times, and a brother is born for
adversity.

PROVERBS 17:17

There is one positive thing that comes from loss, and that's that
you get to find out who your true friends are. During a time of
disappointment or grief, true friends are easy to spot. They're
the ones who will stand beside you no matter how uncomfortable things get. They may not speak a single word, but you can't
help hearing what their hearts are saying. True friends understand your grief and help you through each stage of it. They can
sense both when you need to be alone and when being alone is
the last thing you want. Yes, true friends are easy to spot.

Unfortunately, a loss will also shine a light on friends of the
other kind. Friends who don't understand or care that your
world has changed; they just want everything to return to normal in their own world, and they want it now. Not when you're
ready, but when they're ready. They want you to "hurry up and
snap out of it because you're just too depressing to be around."

It's hard to understand friends like that, isn't it? Don't they
realize that you, too, would like nothing more than for life to
get back to normal? But life is anything but normal right now.

Your whole world has changed, and adjusting to that change has to come on your own timeline, not someone else's.

So don't let "disappearing friends" or even impatient ones make you feel guilty for grieving. Friends like this are emotionally shallow. They've probably never experienced a major loss in their own lives, so they can't possibly know how it feels. If they had gone through a loss, they would know what compassion and understanding are all about, and would give you a little more of them.

Imagine what the world would be like if it were full of this kind of person. It wouldn't be a very nice place, would it? God knows that, and that could very well be one of the reasons He allows certain losses and disappointments to come into our lives. He wants the world to have enough people who will understand when someone is hurting, who can be that shoulder to lean on—not just because it's the right thing to do, but because they've been there themselves.

If you've had to say goodbye to a parent, as soon as you work through your grief, you'll know how to be there for someone else who has lost a parent. If your parents have divorced, you'll know how to encourage someone else whose parents are divorcing. If you've recently moved to a new state or country, you'll be the first one to make friends with that other student who just enrolled at your school. You'll have compassion. You'll be understanding. Why? Because you've been there. Life is tough. We all need each other. And the best person to talk to when you're hurting is someone who has walked the path before you.

So, be there for others. Let them learn what you've learned. You appreciate each and every day of your life. You don't take your friendships for granted, or anything else, for that matter.

You savor each day and live it to the fullest. And you know how to be there for a friend, just like your true friends were there for you. Whether you wanted it or not, you've received quite an extensive life lesson. Share it with the rest of us.

When the World Goes on After Your World Crumbles

"It seems like it was just yesterday," cried Abigail as she remembered her father. Abigail's father had committed suicide only two years before, and she was still having a difficult time coping. Her seven brothers and sisters seemed to be doing just fine, on the surface at least, but life was anything but easy for Abigail. Her world had been turned upside down.

After her father's suicide, Abigail's mom decided to send her to a home school where part of the curriculum included attending a private school two days a week. That's where I met her.

Whenever Abigail would come to my school, she'd sit at a small table all by herself. For more than half the year, she was treated as an outcast, an outsider to our already established school cliques; and I didn't think that I, of all people, was about to accept her.

It wasn't until our Christmas party that year that I really got to see the real Abigail—wounded and needing a friend more than anything. I had brought her to the party because she didn't have a ride. We talked on the way home that night, and the more I learned about her, the more I could see how deep her pain was. Eventually, she trusted me enough to share her hurt and vivid memory of her father's suicide.

"A policeman came into the restaurant where we were eating and talked to my mom. Mom explained that she needed to go with him and that someone else would be taking us home. I knew something was wrong and that my mother wasn't just going for a friendly ride. When we got home, Mom came into the living room, her eyes red from crying, and told us our father had killed himself. That was the worst night of my life ... of all our lives."

As Abigail continued to share her deepest hurts, I realized that whatever problems I might have were miniscule compared to hers. I felt helpless to offer any comfort. What could I say that would make her pain go away? I didn't understand why anyone would have to go through something like this. And to go through it alone seemed more than a human being could bear. I knew she needed God's help, but that sounded too simplistic. So I came up with some pat answers that didn't really do her any good, but somehow made me feel better. After all, what if I did tell her that what she needed was God, and she rejected that? What if she said something like "I already tried that," or "Just look what your God has done—my dad's dead!" No, I couldn't risk that.

Yet in time there came a point where I couldn't provide simplistic answers anymore. Abigail was hurting and needed real answers, not superficial ones. So, I told her what I should have told her months before—that she needed God's help more than mine. That I was her friend, but He was her hope. And you know what? Abigail listened as though she had been waiting all along for me to tell her that! And God did help Abigail. He may not do the things that we expect Him to do, but in the end, everything always works out for good.

When I finally quit worrying about how Abigail was going to respond to God's love and just showed it to her instead, she came to learn what I had known all along—that God is our comfort when we don't have answers, and He'll be our friend when our world crumbles around us and we find ourselves sitting all alone at a table with nothing but questions.

Melody Dunning
Age 13

Shared joy is double joy. Shared sorrow is half sorrow.

Swedish proverb

As we go through life,
friendship is the most precious
treasure we can find.

Haiku by Diantha Ain

When a Friend Keeps Your Secrets

About a year ago I began getting terrible pains in my abdomen. My doctor prescribed some medication for me and scheduled a series of medical tests to determine the origin of the pain.

Maybe I didn't need to be, but I was embarrassed about the whole ordeal and didn't want anyone to know. After several weeks of pain and discomfort, though, I finally confided in my friend, Ashley. I knew I could count on Ashley to keep my confidence. She was the kind of friend who would never reveal your secrets, even if she got mad at you. Everyone should have a friend like Ashley, or as I call her, "Catt."

Catt prayed for me whenever I needed it. She stood by my side on my good days, and on the bad ones, too. Even when others tried to get her to break her promise to me, or talked about me behind my back, Catt was steadfastly loyal. She was a friend of her word.

I still have the abdominal pains, and doctors have yet to find the problem, but Catt's friendship has helped to ease my pain just a little. She's been an example of Jesus to me, a friend who can be trusted.

Rheyma
Age 13

God sends us angels
to guide our footsteps along
the straight and narrow.

Haiku by Diantha Ain

When Your Best Friend Needs You

It was the summer before our senior year. My best friend and I were seventeen. We both had boyfriends we were crazy about and times were good. Melissa was the type of friend you find only once in your life, a forever friend, one you know will be with you no matter where life leads you.

One hot July night our lives led us somewhere we hadn't expected. What happened that night changed the course of our friendship and lives forever.

As on many summer weekends, my boyfriend and I had plans to go out. Melissa had her own plans to go to dinner with her boyfriend, Tony (who had just asked her to marry him) and a few other couples.

During the evening we all connected at a local party, but then went our separate ways.

The rest of the night is ingrained in my mind clear as glass. I got home about one o'clock in the morning and went to bed. I had barely been asleep an hour before I was awakened by a frantic telephone call. It was Melissa.

"Melia," she screamed, "Tony's dead!"

Tony and Melissa, along with two other people, had been in a terrible accident. Their car was hit head-on by a lady who was on her way home after drinking at a nearby bar. Her judgment was impaired, and Tony may have had a beer that night himself. At that moment, however, we weren't thinking about who was at fault. All we could think about was the fact that Tony, our friend, whom we had just seen laughing and having a great time, was now gone. Tony was a guy who was loved by everyone. I had known him since seventh grade and had even fallen in love with him myself, long before Melissa did. I don't think you could know Tony and not fall in love with him.

I immediately asked my dad to take me down to the hospital to be with Melissa. I found out that Tony had died upon impact. Melissa miraculously survived, but had broken thirteen bones in her back and pelvis. It was going to be a long road to recovery for Melissa and me—physically for her, and emotionally for both of us.

How would I handle the loss of a dear friend, as well as help my best friend recover from such a traumatic blow? I did what I could. Since Melissa was still in the hospital and unable to attend Tony's memorial service, I was her eyes and ears, not only for the funeral, but for whatever else was going on outside the world of her hospital room.

Melissa was flat on her back for a month and a half before progressing to a wheelchair for a month, and finally, crutches. But through it all, our friendship grew deeper as we faced emotions we had never imagined we would have to face.

We had all changed. Melissa had changed. I had changed. Our entire senior class had been changed by the tragedy, and each one of us was handling it in our own way. Some stopped going to parties, some got angry, some appreciated their senior year and their friends just a little more.

I believe God puts people in our path for a reason. Perhaps Melissa had come into my life, and I into hers, just for that very night—so I could be what God knew she was going to need ... a friend.

Melia Munro

What we have done for ourselves alone dies with us; what we have done for others and the world remains and is immortal.

Albert Pike

When They Push You Away

When one of my closest friends slipped into a state of depression, it was one of the most difficult times in my life. She closed up and wouldn't tell me what was going on like she used to, she resented everything I said or did, and no matter how I tried, I just couldn't reach her. I tried to give her space, figuring that's what she wanted, but I managed only a physical distance, not an emotional one. She was still my friend, and even though she was pushing me away, I couldn't turn my back on her.

I thought I had lost her when I discovered she was, at only eleven years old, already abusing alcohol and into other self-destructive behaviors. It hurt me so much inside because she was the person in whom I had confided, and now she was shoving me out of her life. We were best friends. But all I could do was pray, let her know I was there for her, and of course, continue to love her unconditionally. In the end, my faithfulness proved worth it all.

Sometimes there aren't easy answers to the things we face in this life, but I don't want my friendship to be one of the things my friend has to question. In other words, even when people want you to say goodbye, sometimes you just have to hang on and not let go. Real friends just do that.

Anonymous
Age 16

The difference between "involvement" and "commitment" is like a ham-and-eggs breakfast: the chicken was "involved"; the pig was "committed."

Source Unknown

When Differences Don't Matter

When President Ronald Reagan was about to undergo surgery to remove a bullet that had entered his lung during an assassination attempt on March 30, 1981, he looked up at the doctor who was going to operate and said, "I hope you're a Republican."

The doctor answered, "Today, Mr. President, we're all Republicans."

A word aptly spoken is like apples of gold in settings of silver.

PROVERBS 25:11

When You Have to Learn to Trust Again

The Second World War ended on V-Day in 1945. For me, it finally ended during a Christmas party for orphans of war, given months later by a group of American soldiers in a London subway.

I'll never forget that day, as long as I live. The subway was brilliantly lit—a million candles changed the gloomy depths that had served as my home for so long into a magical wonderland. Music and laughter replaced the sounds of bombs and gunfire. Yet I was still afraid. The nightly blackouts had led me to believe that safety could be found only in darkness. Light meant jeopardy—it was something to avoid at all cost, for it brought the terrifying warplanes.

Although I was only six years old at the time, I couldn't help but wonder what the soldiers at this party were thinking. Were they trying to get us all killed? I'd heard the war was over, but as a child who had known only death and destruction, I had no real understanding of what peace was, what it looked and felt like.

I had lost it all in the war—my mother, my father, my home, and everyone and everything I had known and loved, as well as my childhood. The war had taken my whole world from me. So what was there to celebrate? All I wanted to do was tear down the pretty lights and party decorations, and make it all go away.

A young soldier, seeing me crouched in a dark corner in terror, came and sat by my side. He gently explained that the war really was over, and that I had nothing more to fear. Yet when all you've known is loss, it's not easy to open up and risk losing again, to become vulnerable.

But the soldier didn't give up. He took my hand and pulled me into the light, explaining that he was my guardian angel, sent by God to protect me. He stayed by my side the whole night. I can't remember his face or even his name, but I have never forgotten his kindness.

I've experienced many losses in the years that have followed, both small and great, and it seems with each loss that fear has returned, sending me scurrying for cover and seeking to find safety once again in isolated darkness.

Yet as certain as the fear returns, so does the memory of a kind, young soldier. A soldier who temporarily forgot his own losses from the war to reach out to a frightened young girl. When he did, the painful memories and sorrow lifted just a little bit from both of us.

Margaret Brownley
Author

A hero is a man who does what he can.

Roman Rolland

A friend is known when needed.

Saudi Arabian Proverb

A Step Toward Healing

Think of someone who was there for you during a recent loss. Have you written or called to thank that person? If not, why not do it right now?

Reaching out to others is a way to begin our own healing. Can you think of someone in your life who might need a word of encouragement from you? Do something this week to help lift that person's spirit just a little. You'll be amazed at how giving away encouragement will encourage you.

Chapter 11

Saying Goodbye to a Pet

Are not two sparrows sold for a penny? Yet not one of
them will fall to the ground apart from the will of your
Father.

MATTHEW 10:29

Do you know animals are special to God? If they weren't, He
would have told Noah to build a life raft just for himself and his
family—but He didn't. He told him to build a huge ark and
load two of every kind of animal on board. (And to think I once
got in trouble for trying to sneak one puppy on vacation with us!)

I'm sure God told Noah to bring along a whole zoo on his
trip because He was pleased with His creation, He wanted each
species to survive the flood, and He loved them. I wonder if
Noah didn't have a few favorites among his floating wild animal
kingdom. Did his favorite pooch follow him around the inside
deck? Would one of the cats plop itself down right on top of the
map Noah was trying to read? Noah had to have had a special
relationship with a few of the critters, because you can't live that
long with animals and not develop some sort of attachment.

We had our dog, Chipper, for over seventeen years. That's
119 in dog years. We got her as a puppy. She was being given
away in front of a grocery store, so we stopped, picked her up

from the box, took a look into her blue—yes, blue—eyes, and immediately became attached to the beautiful border collie mix. We decided to bring her home with us, and it was a good decision. Chipper turned out to be gentle, loving, obedient, and not afraid to make bold fashion statements. Our boys loved dressing her up in various superhero costumes—Spiderman, Superman (complete with cape), Batman, Wonder Woman, and whatever other superhero they could think of. Chipper didn't mind, and was the star in countless of our home movies. She loved playing with the kids, and my husband and I often jokingly referred to her as our sons' "second mother."

When Chipper's health began to fail, the veterinarian suggested we put her to sleep. We didn't want to do it, but he felt it was the most humane course of action, since at 119 years of age, much of her body wasn't functioning properly. So we agreed, and said goodbye to an old friend. To this day, our kids still remember Chipper. No matter how many pets they've had since, none of them will ever replace Chipper.

If you've recently lost a pet, know that your need to mourn that loss is real. Know, too, that God understands our love for our pets. After all, He created them. And He didn't let Noah leave them behind, either.

When You Don't Want to Face It

It didn't hit me until I heard she had passed. It was then that I realized how much Saun had meant to me. Saun was more than just a dog. She was an important part of my life. She was family. Saun was as devoted to me and my siblings as our parents were.

I would even sing to Saun just before we'd fall asleep, cuddled up together.

As I got older, I didn't have that much time for her. I still loved her, but I couldn't give her the attention that I had once given her. I was now a teenager and needed my space because I was busy "growing up." Saun should have known that.

While I was busy growing up, Saun was busy growing old. Soon, she became very sick, but rather than face what was happening, I denied every feeling I ever had for her. I couldn't bear to think that Saun was dying. She had spent her life willingly giving me her faithful love and affection. Now, she needed mine. But I couldn't bear to watch her suffer, so I protected myself by putting up a shield around my emotions, a shield that protected me, but separated us.

When my Mom called to tell me they were going to have to put Saun to sleep and asked if I wanted to be there with the family, I said no. I passed it off as no big deal, and even though I did cry a little after hanging up the telephone, I quickly snapped out it, convincing myself that she was just a very sick dog who was suffering badly, and we could always get another one.

Now, years later, I still feel guilty, knowing that I let her die thinking that I no longer cared. Sure, I protected myself from pain, but I caused my "best friend" so much heartache and confusion in the process. Losing hurts, but sometimes we need to realize how much added pain we bring on the situation because of our fears and denial.

I love you, Saun. Thanks for being there for me every time I needed you, even when it wasn't easy.

Eunice Rising

When There's Nothing You Can Do but Trust

Just a few weeks before, she had been breathing strongly and steadily. Now, she labored for every breath. Her eyes had lost their bright glow. Instead of the healthy, sleek, powerful horse I had once known, Melody lay before me, a helpless figure of skin and bones.

As I watched her that day, my mind wandered back to the day she was born. I was the first person to touch her soft muzzle. She was beautiful, and she was mine. I also remembered halter-breaking her, then later, putting a saddle on her for the first time. I rode her across the hay meadow—how fast she could run! I had her every move, look, and trick memorized. The first three years of her life had been the happiest three of mine. She had made me, an insecure young teen, feel needed.

But now it was time to say goodbye. Melody was foundering, which is a term used when a horse eats so much feed that its body can't handle it. I was only sixteen years of age, but I was trying my best to act mature and brave in the face of her certain death. For a month and a half I had fought for her life with all that medicine could do, but it wasn't enough, and now I was forced to admit defeat. Overwhelmed with a sadness I had never experienced before, I bent down next to Melody in the stall and stroked her copper-colored neck, whispering softly to her, then scratched her ear one last time. As I left the barn with tears rolling down my cheeks, the veterinarian came in and gave her a shot, and within moments, Melody was gone.

It may sound silly, but losing Melody was like losing my dearest friend. She was a dream come true for me and, no matter how hard I tried, I couldn't understand why God had allowed her to die. He could've made her well, but He didn't.

As painful as Melody's death was, though, I soon saw good coming from it. Within the next several months, I began to realize that Melody's death might have been a way to prepare me for the rest of my life. You see, the night that Melody got into the feed, my family was singing at a church a few hours away from our hometown. Singing was another dream of mine. I felt called into the music ministry, but I wasn't sure how I would be able to manage traveling and taking care of a horse at the same time. After Melody's death, more doors began opening for our family to sing. It may not have been my will for Melody to die, but as the Bible promises, good was coming from it.

My faith in God is stronger than ever, because I have experienced His perfect will unfolding in my life. My job is to trust Him, and to trust that whatever happens, God will cause something positive and good to come from it.

Elisabeth Graves

When You Can't Forgive Yourself

I dearly love animals, especially dogs. I guess that is why I want to be a veterinarian when I grow up.

Rascal was one of my favorite dogs. He was the runt of the litter, and I felt it was my duty to protect him. We got Rascal and his brother, Maxx, when they were barely six weeks old. What fun they were! There's nothing like watching two puppies grow up together, play together, and poke and nudge their way to their food dish.

When the puppies were about three months old, Maxx broke

his leg. For the first time, we had to separate Maxx and Rascal, because Rascal would want to play and Maxx had to stay off his leg as much as possible. So Maxx stayed in the house and Rascal stayed out.

That same week, my grandparents arrived from New Mexico for a long-awaited visit. Since I got to see my grandparents for only one week a year, I wanted to spend as much time with them as possible.

I was so busy and excited their first day here that I lost all track of time. I forgot all about Rascal and how hot it was starting to become outside. I didn't find a spare second that morning to take Rascal any water.

When I finally remembered and went outside to check on him, the scene I found was one that to this day still haunts me. Rascal was lying on his side and wouldn't, or rather couldn't, respond when I talked to him. Sensing he was dehydrated, I quickly dumped every drop of water in the watering can over him, but he still didn't respond. In a panic, I quickly picked him up and carried him inside the house, then called our veterinarian for instructions.

The instructions didn't do me any good, because a few minutes later Rascal died of heatstroke. I held him in my arms and cried until I couldn't cry any more. I loved Rascal so much, but the most horrible pain was the guilt that I felt. I knew that if I had paid attention, this never would have happened. Rascal would still be here today.

I can't change the past. What happened, happened. The only thing I can do is learn from it and share my story with others. I still love animals, but I've learned that love comes with responsibility. Whatever pet we choose to have, whether it's a dog, cat, hamster, bird, or fish, they depend on us to take care of them.

Rascal knew I loved him. He knew I would never purposely do anything to harm him. But good intentions aren't enough. Unfortunately, I had to learn that truth the hard way. And even though I take comfort in the fact that God forgives me and Rascal forgives me, what I really need to do now is forgive myself.

Erin Duffy
Age 14

When You Have to Move On

When I was eleven years old, I had a cat named Gracie Mae. She was my first pet. One night, for some reason, I kept having this feeling that Gracie needed to sleep inside, instead of in the garage. But I ignored it.

Early the next morning, I was awakened by my mother and brother. They were both crying as they explained that when Gracie had been let out of the garage at 5:30 A.M., a couple of dogs had gotten hold of her and killed her.

For days I sat around the house, just staring into the distance and crying. I felt so bad I couldn't eat. All I could think about was my cat and how much I missed her. Also, I couldn't help but feel guilty, knowing that had I listened to that inner warning and kept my cat inside, she would still be here.

Thankfully, through the love and encouragement of my family and some wonderful friends, and of course, God, I eventually was able to deal with the loss.

I'm thirteen now and have a new cat. I still love and miss

Gracie, but I'm bonding with my new cat and I'm moving on with my life. And even though Gracie's death was difficult, it taught me an important lesson—that life is fragile and precious for all of us, even animals.

Danielle Clark
Age 13

When They Loved You Unconditionally

In the fifth grade I fell in love with the perfect companion— Mojo, a gentle Heinz 57 puppy with a black mask on her face and enough charm to win over even the most hardened cat lover. She was my right-hand dog for fifteen years.

In high school I was involved in a communications class debate called "The Ideal Pet: Cats or Dogs?" I gave my reasons why I felt dogs might be superior to cats (I wasn't really serious, but it made for a fun debate), and at just the right moment a friend brought Mojo through the door. She came skidding toward me on the linoleum, leaping joyfully, licking my face and refusing to leave my side. Within minutes the entire class was filing by, saying nice things, even the cat lovers. Whether or not my theory is true (and even I don't truly believe it), I won the debate that day. Paws down.

I think one reason I was so close to Mojo was that one particular day when I came home from school feeling lower than dirt. It had been an awful day. A detention had ruined tomorrow's plans, my volleyball score had plummeted, and my math marks weren't adding up. To make matters worse, I hated my haircut. But Mojo didn't mind. She met me at the door with her tongue ready. She ran in circles, leaping in the air, and licked my face as if it were aging cheese. Mojo didn't care where I'd been or what I'd done. She didn't mind my haircut, or what anyone thought or said. She just loved me. I guess there's no psychiatrist in the world as good as a puppy licking your face.

After fifteen years of companionship, she lost her battle with old age and died. It's hard to believe how much a little animal can mean to a kid. But I cried like I've never cried since.

"Will there be dogs in heaven?" someone asked me recently.

"Absolutely," I replied. "There's nothing in the Bible to indicate otherwise." And if any dog on earth would be there, it would be Mojo.

Phil Callaway
Author, humorist

When You Have to Let Go

Sam was the horse I had dreamed of owning ever since I was a young boy. I bought the half-Arabian, half-quarter horse when he was only a colt, and once he was old enough, I looked forward to riding him every chance I got.

When Sam was around five years old, circumstances were such that I could no longer keep him. I decided to donate him to a youth organization in the mountains in Southern California. It was beautiful there, and the leaders assured me that I could visit Sam and ride him whenever I wanted.

One day as I was preparing to drive my young daughter, Priscilla, to the mountains to visit Sam, I decided I should telephone the organization to let them know we were coming. That's when they gave me the unfortunate news.

"Didn't anyone call you?" the voice on the other end of the line inquired.

"No, why?" I asked, sensing what was coming was anything but good news.

The person went on to explain that they had been training Sam to be a packhorse for the group. He had been on a routine trail ride with a team of horses. All the horses had been tied together, negotiating their way along a rough, narrow trail. Sam, who was always a little skittish, had tried to step over a ledge, then had suddenly reared back, lost his footing, and fallen over the side. They had tried to save him, but his weight was pulling the other horses down with him. They had had no choice but to cut the line and let Sam go.

At first, I was mad—mad that they had placed Sam in a situation like that since they already knew he was an apprehensive horse, mad that they had cut the line and let him fall to his death, and mad that I had had to find out the way I did.

After awhile, though, I began to understand that cutting Sam loose was the only thing they could have done. It was either that or the whole team of horses would have been lost.

I still miss Sam, but I'll be forever grateful to him for fulfilling that childhood dream of mine. I finally did get to have my horse. I may never get the opportunity to own another one, but I did get to have Sam. We made a lot of great memories together, Sam and I. And when you think about it, I guess you could say he died a hero. That's fitting. He already was one to me.

Lee Ferren

A Step Toward Healing

Do something today that will be a special remembrance to your pet. (Make a pet photo album, tell someone a funny story about your pet, make a collage of pictures of your pet for your wall, or do something else that will help you remember the good times you shared with your pet.)

Obviously, another pet will never replace the pet you've lost, but as a step toward healing, why not volunteer to help a friend with his or her pet? Or visit your local animal shelter or pet store and share your love. I'm sure there are plenty of ownerless pets out there who are feeling just as lonely as you are and would love to have a friend, even if it's just for a few moments.

Chapter 12

Tough Decisions

For I am the Lord, your God, who takes hold of your right
hand and says to you, Do not fear; I will help you.

ISAIAH 41:13

Life is full of decisions. Some are easy, like choosing whether to
order the cheeseburger or the double-decker liverwurst sand-
wich for lunch. Other decisions are far more difficult. They're
decisions that may affect your life forever. Sometimes the hardest decisions have to be made when you're the least ready for
them. You may have to face a very adult decision while you're
still a teenager—like giving a baby up for adoption, or deciding
whether to have a risky, possibly lifesaving surgery, or choosing
which friends to keep and which aren't very good for you.

When faced with a tough decision, the number-one thing
you should do is pray for God's guidance. The next thing you
should do is look ahead at the consequences of each of your
choices. Which path is best for you, and for all concerned, in the
long run?

It would be so much easier if every decision we ever had to
make was made for us, wouldn't it?

"You don't want to wear that outfit. Wear this one instead."

"Diet or regular? She'll have the diet."

"What college does he want to go to? Why, Clown College, of course."

All right, maybe that last choice wouldn't be so difficult to make yourself, but here's my point: What's right for someone else might not be right for you. What's right for your mother or father, your uncle or aunt, your best friend, your neighbor, or your mailman, might not be your best choice. We live in a free country. You're allowed to choose. But with those choices come responsibilities. And consequences. So, think of your future. Pray and make wise decisions. And even when you don't make the right choice—and there will be times when you won't—learn from those wrong decisions. Life is a great teacher. We fail only when we don't learn those history lessons.

When People Let You Down

This past year there has been a lot of heartache and confusion in my life. I have been let down by many people I thought I respected and trusted. My church went through a very difficult split. To be perfectly honest, it was one of the most testing times in my life. Why was this happening to this church I so dearly loved? As hard as my family and I tried to mend things, the repairs just didn't hold. After awhile, I was afraid to run into certain people. I felt uncomfortable and alone in a place where I had always felt comfortable and at home.

Through endless hours of tears and prayer, we finally reached the conclusion that God wanted us to leave that church. I felt as though I were being torn apart. Still, throughout all this mess, I could feel God working in my life. That was the only thing that got me through those moments when I felt like giving up.

Looking for a new church was especially depressing. Would we ever find a church we loved as much as we had our old one? All I could do was surrender, and give God control of a situation that was so out of control.

Whatever difficult situation you may be facing, give it over to God. He won't overlook your obedience. Although it took a couple of months, one Sunday my family and I happened to stumble upon a church which we now call home. And would you believe this? I'm happier here than I've ever been at church! The friends I've met have helped me to grow spiritually, and I'm now reaping the benefits of a closer walk with Jesus.

If you don't know it already, you'll find out sooner or later that people will let you down. Life is going to let you down. Jesus didn't promise a perfect life for us, but He did promise to be with us—always.

Anonymous

When Your Dream Comes to an End

Two years ago when I was fourteen and living as an MK (missionary kid) in Tegucigalpa, Honduras, my parents received a call from a lady who wanted to know if we were interested in adopting a little girl. We immediately said yes.

I had dreamed of having a little sister ever since my brother had been born, when I was six years old. I love my brother, but I had always wanted to have a sister someday.

I still remember the night we went to pick up my new sister

at the home of a friend of the baby's mother. She was so beautiful and tiny. At five months of age, she could barely hold her head up. We were told that the mother had been unable to afford to feed her anything more than rice water and tea for the past three months.

Even though I had desperately wanted a sister, I have to admit I was jealous of her at first because I thought she would take my place in the family. But the more I looked into those bright eyes, the more I fell in love with her. I was there when she took her first steps. I was there when she said her first word. She called me Nini most of the time, and I loved it.

In January 2000 we were due to return to the States so I could go to high school. But as we were preparing to leave, we received a call from the mother's friend, saying she wanted the baby back. By Honduran law we had to give her back. She was fifteen months old at the time. I woke her up from her nap and got her dressed in her little pink checkered dress and tights with ruffles on the bottom. I made sure she had her favorite toys with her, and that everything she needed to take with her was ready. I felt like Moses' sister during all of this. I cried until I could no longer shed a tear, then cried some more. I gave her one last hug and kiss before sending her off with my dad and brother to her birth mother. It was a heartbreaking separation.

It has been over a year now since we left Honduras, and I still miss my sister greatly. We haven't received any word about her since last year, when my dad called there and the birth mother's friend asked what "Nini" meant, because my sister was always saying that.

It was difficult to let go, but I know that she is in God's hands. I don't know if I'll ever see her again, and it hurts to think that she might not remember me in the years to come. But I know I'll never stop loving her. She was my shooting star, a brilliant, wonderful light that passed through my life only briefly, and my life will never be the same because of her.

It's like Jeremiah says in chapter 29, verse 11: "For I know the plans I have for you. Plans to prosper you, and not to harm you. Plans to give you a future and a hope." Even shooting stars are in God's plan. They have a purpose. Someday we'll find out what that purpose is, when we get to heaven and God reveals to us His greater plan. So until then, Cassie, know that you're loved.

Your big sister
Age 16

Saying Goodbye When God Has a Better Plan

My daughter, Jamie, was seventeen years old and pregnant. After much prayer and counsel, we felt it was best for Jamie and the teenage father not to marry. Even though I was embarrassed for our friends to know that my daughter had gotten pregnant out of wedlock, and I certainly didn't want others to think we had liberal views on premarital sex, I still felt confident that this was the way the Lord was leading us.

Our dear friend, Lisa English, had involved us in Mercy Ministries years before. Founded by Nancy Alcorn, Mercy Ministries is a wonderful organization that provides help for unwed mothers. Both Nancy and Lisa believed that Jamie would benefit greatly from going to live at the Mercy Ministries home in Monroe, Louisiana. While there, she would receive medical care, room and board, and good counsel in making the difficult decision as to whether to keep the baby or place him or her for adoption. It had to be Jamie's decision, of course, but she had heard about the long list of good families requesting babies, and she also knew that at her young age it would be difficult to take on the responsibilities of raising a child.

During a routine medical exam one week before Jamie was to leave for the home in Monroe, Jamie asked the doctor about the results of her ultrasound. When the doctor called the lab for the results, he became more than a little concerned.

"There seems to be an abnormality here," he said, matter-of-factly.

Abnormality? I held my breath—and the edge of the doctor's desk—and thought, *Could things get any worse?* I reached over to take Jamie's hand.

The doctor told us that the test indicated Jamie's baby had Down's syndrome, although further tests would need to be performed to verify it. I turned toward my sweet daughter to see how, at seventeen years of age, she was handling such a heartbreaking announcement. I tried my best to disguise it, but she must have read the fear on my face because tears began to stream down her face.

The doctor instructed us to immediately go to Vanderbilt Hospital for further testing. Bewildered and crying, Jamie and I got in the car and drove there. On the way, we called loved ones and asked them to pray. I called our friend and Nashville "Granny" Vestal Goodman, my Bible teacher Linda Styll, and Lisa English. Then, it was on to out-of-town loved ones, including my dear mother in California. Everyone assured us they'd pray, and those who could, promised to meet us at the hospital.

By the time we arrived at Vanderbilt, a large crowd of friends had already gathered. Vestal's son and daughter-in-law held Jamie's hand as medical technicians performed the amniocentesis, a test that would determine whether the baby did in fact have Down's syndrome.

The test was positive.

The doctor asked Jamie and me to follow him into his private office. I asked Lisa English to join us.

"Jamie," he began, "this is very bad news, and I can't think of a worse situation than an unmarried teenager with a Down's syndrome baby. You are now nearly five months pregnant and have only a few days left to have a legal abortion in the state of Tennessee."

Without even looking toward Lisa or me, Jamie told the doctor that she could never do that. You could feel the atmosphere in the room change from fear to confidence, from questioning "Why?" to believing God had an answer. Mary Chapman, the mother of entertainer Gary Chapman and one of the wisest women I know, once told us that whenever we felt defeated, we should just say, "OK, Lord, what are you going to do with this?"

So, from that moment on, that's what we did. We believed God had an ultimate plan, even if we didn't see it yet.

Nancy Alcorn went ahead and made the arrangements for Jamie to go to Mercy Ministries in Monroe. We still weren't sure what was going to happen with the baby, since it was now going to be a special needs baby. The adoption option didn't seem realistic, since "special needs" babies are often difficult to place.

But that was our limited human thinking. God had other

plans. Unbeknownst to us, a family had been waiting to adopt just this kind of "special needs" infant.

The mother was a pediatrician, the father a musician, and there were four sisters and a brother all ready to accept him into their hearts and home. When we didn't have the answers, God did. This wonderful family adopted little "Cody," and he is a blessing to all who know him.

Relinquishing a baby is painful, but knowing Cody is with the family that God had already prepared for him to be with made the decision so much easier for all of us.

Judy Spencer Nelon

A Step Toward Healing

What's the most difficult decision you've ever had to make?

Tough decisions require a lot of thought. You should pray about them, weigh all sides of the issue, and then make your best choice. If you're facing a tough decision right now, make a list of the positive and the negative sides of each of your choices.

Chapter 13

Saying Goodbye to a Relationship

He heals the brokenhearted and binds up their wounds.
He determines the number of the stars and calls them
each by name. Great is our Lord and mighty in power; his
understanding has no limit.

PSALM 147:3-5

Whenever I talk to someone who is heartbroken over a breakup with his or her boyfriend or girlfriend, I share the story of my husband and me. Russ and I began dating when I was fifteen and he was nineteen. Just before I graduated from high school, we got engaged. I was excited, but neither of us had dated very much, and I wasn't sure if we were making the right decision. We both had plenty of time ahead of us. Did I really want to get married that young?

So I broke off the engagement. It was heartbreaking, but it seemed like it was the best thing to do at the time.

Three and a half months later, after one of my close girl-friends who had encouraged the breakup started dating him, Russ and I got back together. As painful as the breakup was, though, I'm still convinced it was good for our relationship. It made me know beyond a shadow of a doubt that he was the one for me, and vice versa. Luckily, we both came to that realization before it was too late.

If I learned anything from the situation, I learned that just because a relationship seems to be over, that doesn't mean it's really over. Whether it's a relationship with a friend, a relative, or a boyfriend or girlfriend, there's a possibility that it can eventually be restored. The breakup also showed me that you can't always trust the advice you receive from others. Sometimes instead of having your best interest in mind, they have their own. And I learned, too, that if you listen, God will let you know both when you're in His will and when you're about to make a huge step out of it. He showed me that I was throwing away a blessing that He had intended for me. Thankfully, I paid attention and changed my direction.

Yes, it's hard to say goodbye to a relationship, but when you trust God to guide you, you'll make sure the right relationships remain a part of your life.

When Friends Choose Sides

Throughout my eighth grade and high school freshman year, I had a large group of friends, about eleven of us. I'm still not quite sure what it was about, but one day Kellie and another one of the girls, Maggie (not their real names), got into a huge argument, big enough that the group split and took up sides. Kellie's closest friends went along with her and believed everything they were told, while only two others stayed loyal to Maggie.

I found myself in the middle, wanting to remain friends with everyone. After all, their disagreement had nothing to do with me. Besides, Kellie and Maggie had always been best friends, so

I figured it was just a matter of time before they made up and everything returned to normal.

Kellie, however, wouldn't let me straddle the fence. She didn't want me hanging around her because I was also hanging around Maggie. The friends who had sided with Kellie also didn't want me around, because I wasn't supporting Kellie.

Maggie and the couple of friends who had maintained their friendship with her were the only ones who didn't put a stipulation on my friendship. They didn't care about who I hung out with, whether it was Maggie or Kellie. They simply appreciated my friendship.

To this day, almost two years later, the feud continues. Kellie's group still doesn't talk to any of Maggie's friends.

Did all this hurt? Of course it did! I tried to "play both sides," to maintain both friendships, but in the end it didn't work. Something like this, though, really makes you thank God for the friends you do have, the ones who don't consider your friendship disposable.

I helped Maggie out in a difficult time when most others didn't care, and it cost me some friends. But like they say, true friends walk in when others walk out!

Maegen Arbuckle
Age 16

The games people play
with other folks' emotions
have no real winners.

Haiku by Diantha Ain

When You Feel Left Behind

When Pastor Mitch (not his real name) first came to our church, I liked him immediately. He had a great sense of humor and also had a beautiful little girl whom I got to baby-sit regularly. But more important than that, while previous youth pastors had always seemed to see us as a "youth group," Pastor Mitch envisioned us as a "youth ministry."

We weren't merely a group of teenagers he had to keep entertained. He challenged us to seek God, to build a strong relationship with Him, and to have a servant's heart. He organized missions outings and events that would strengthen us spiritually and bond us together as a group. He had big ideas and lots of enthusiasm. He even went beyond our church, reaching out to the community, and treated us all as equals, regardless of age, race, or church background. I was impressed with what he was trying to do and wanted desperately to be a part of it.

Unfortunately, however, not everyone was impressed with what Pastor Mitch was attempting to do. Some of the youth and their families didn't like being challenged. They didn't want to reach out to others or draw closer as a group. They wanted to have fun, and it was Pastor Mitch's job, they figured, to arrange it for them.

Even though very few people supported Pastor Mitch, my family and I decided that we would stay strong, and we prayed that God would change the hearts of the people. Whenever it became necessary, I would defend Pastor Mitch to the other kids, even at the risk of losing my own friendships.

One day, Pastor Mitch told my dad that he had decided to move away and enroll in a school in a different state to become a Christian counselor. When I heard what his plans were, I didn't take the news very well. It seemed to me that he was just running away, and it seemed as though he didn't care how this might affect those who had done so much to defend him. To him, it seemed like it was no big deal.

I tried to take comfort in the fact that we could still keep in touch, but Pastor Mitch has been gone for three months now and I'm still waiting to hear something from him.

I lost a youth pastor, but for me it was an even greater loss than it seemed on the surface. I lost someone in whom I had believed; someone I had thought would stand by me, just as I had stood by him. I had thought my family and I were important to him, as lifelong friends, not just until he decided to move on. I felt betrayed, disillusioned, and confused. Not only did I lose a youth pastor, but I lost a friend, a mentor—and I lost hope.

Our family goes to a different church now, but going through this painful situation taught me something. I learned that the Lord is my refuge, not Pastor Mitch or any other youth pastor, youth worker, or Sunday school teacher, or even my parents. It is very important that I remember this throughout my life. God is the one who'll never let me down. He is the one who's promised to never leave me or forsake me. He is the one on whom I need to be leaning.

Jordan Baker
Age 14

Chords that were broken will vibrate once more.

Fanny Crosby

When You Don't Know Why You're Saying Goodbye

When I entered the seventh grade, I found myself at a new school in a completely new town. Even though I didn't know anyone there, I was excited to be in these unfamiliar surroundings, and by the end of the first day I had made a new best friend. We had so much in common, we instantly became great friends. I could tell her things I couldn't imagine telling anyone else. She never judged others, and no matter what I needed to say, I could say it to her.

Over time, though, our friendship began to change. When I started to hang out with some of the other kids at school during our free time, she became distant. Around Thanksgiving, my parents began to home school my siblings and me, and that didn't help our relationship very much either. By Christmas, my "best" friend had turned into someone who would hardly even talk to me. If I called her, she would quickly say she had to go. If I confronted her at school about not wanting to talk to me on the telephone, she would just say she didn't feel well.

I stopped calling her so much, and kind of just backed off. Without either of us really trying to keep what friendship we had going, it quickly died. But the pain remained. When I wasn't invited to her birthday party in February, it really hurt. We never talked again after that, and I ended up moving less than a year later.

To this day, I still wonder why my "best" friend suddenly stopped talking to me. I also wonder why I didn't keep on trying to be friends with her. We were so close at one time. Friends don't suddenly stop being friends without a reason. So there was a reason. We both knew it, and we owed it to each other to explain our actions. Yet, we never offered that explanation. Either our own insecurity or our pride wouldn't let us. Instead, we let a good friendship die. Maybe jealousy killed it. Or gossip. Or who knows what else? The bottom line is that our friendship—if it was real—should have survived. The fact that it didn't means it probably wasn't as real as we thought it was.

I felt a lot of pain when I lost my best friend this way, but I learned a good lesson from the experience. No matter who comes in or out of my life, I'll never be alone, because I'll always have God. I can tell Him anything I want, too, and He'll still be here for me. He's not critical or judgmental, but loving and kind. He won't say he has to go when I want to talk to Him. He won't avoid me or ignore me or pretend we never had a friendship in the first place. And above all else, He'll give me the benefit of the doubt, no matter what He hears from others. That's a friend. That's a best friend. That's God.

Anonymous

You don't develop courage by being happy in your relationships every day. You develop it by surviving difficult times and challenging adversity.

Barbara De Angelis

When Best Friends Part

My best friend and I were together constantly from the time we were both four years old. Even though we were total opposites, we were as close as sisters. We did everything from writing plays to playing soccer games together.

When we were ten, we accidentally overheard her dad talking

on the telephone about relocating. The secret was out: they were moving to Trenton—a whole hour away. We walked around the rest of that day, crying and planning how we would spend our last few weeks together.

My friend and her family moved in April 1997, and the first few weeks that followed were the worst in my entire life. Every day out of habit I would start to dial her old phone number or run down the street toward her house. Every night I cried myself to sleep. The worst part was that she wasn't a Christian, and she had just begun coming to church with me before they moved.

We talked on the phone for at least an hour every day for the first couple of months. Then we would talk once or twice a week. Eventually, our communication slowed down to a couple times a month, then it just stopped altogether. I was at a total loss. I didn't know why, but since we were in the process of moving ourselves at the time, the two changes put together were horrible.

We had to live at my grandmother's house for the entire winter of 1998. Since she lived two hours away from my old neighborhood, I had nobody. Or so I thought. By the time we moved back, I had learned in my loneliness that I could totally rely on God for comfort. He also sent another good friend my way—one of the girls in my youth group.

I haven't seen my best friend in four years now, although we have been communicating some through e-mail. I still miss her, but God has given me people who are strong in Him to ease the hurt. And I'm hoping that through our e-mails and online conversations, I can show my best friend how much God loves her, and that she'll find in Him what I have—the best friend anyone could ever have.

Meggan Worgess
Age 15

In three words I can sum up everything I've learned about life: it goes on.

Harvey Fierstein

When It Hurts Too Much to Stay

I wanted to be married, and everything about Matt seemed to make him the perfect choice for me, except for one thing. Matt has Cystic Fibrosis, or CF as it is called. CF is a genetic disorder that allows mucus to form in the lungs. There are approximately thirty thousand people in the United States living with the disorder, and about twenty-five hundred new cases are diagnosed each year. So far, there isn't any cure for CF, but research continues and there are many new treatments being developed that show promise. Although some people with CF have been known to live into their sixties, the average life expectancy for someone with Cystic Fibrosis is thirty-two years of age. Matt is twenty-three.

Matt and I dated in high school, but back then I didn't really think about his cystic fibrosis. We were young, and who knew if our relationship would last past those teenage years? The day after graduation, I moved to Indiana, so that was the end of our relationship. Or so I thought.

Six years later, while playing around on the Internet, I discovered an e-mail address for Matt. I took a chance and sent him a greeting. By the next day I had a response from him waiting in my on-line mailbox. We talked for a couple of weeks, then he came to visit me in Indianapolis. The minute I opened the door and looked at him, my life changed. For the first time ever, I fell in love.

Matt and I had terrific visits, talking, laughing and reminiscing about our high school days. Even when we were apart, we would talk on the phone or e-mail each other several times a day. Things were going really well, and once again I found myself pushing his disease and his possible limited life span to the back of my head.

But Matt needed me to know about his battle with CF, and so one night on the telephone he began to share about the disease. He asked me how I felt about the fact that he probably wouldn't live past the age of thirty-three. He wanted to know where I thought our relationship could go under the circumstances, knowing that a long-term future was probably not an option.

I told Matt that I was hopeful for a future for us, but I was also seeing the future I wanted for myself slowly evaporating. I wouldn't get to experience the fun of growing old with the man I loved, and children were not probable because most men with CF are sterile.

I sat in my bed that night and cried because I knew that no matter what my decision was, whether I decided to marry him or decided to break it off, I was going to lose him. I was going to lose the first guy I had ever really loved.

I didn't want to choose, so Matt chose for me. Since he lived in Ohio, he decided the distance and the issues of his CF weren't helping our relationship. He figured the best thing for both of us would be to break up. So, as painful as it was, that's what we did.

Although it hasn't been easy, we've remained close friends. I still love Matt a lot, and breaking up with him was one of the most difficult things I've ever had to go through. I also fear that someday that telephone call is going to come, the one that tells me what I don't want to hear. But whether Matt has only a few years left or fifty, I want to be there for him. If not as his wife, then most certainly as his friend.

Krista Laughner

When You Lose Something You Never Had

My father was an alcoholic and absent dad. Even so, my childhood memories are, for the most part, pleasant ones. My mother was a strong individual and was the force that maintained a home and safe haven for us children. Even though she has never made a strong statement of faith, she has strengths that have caused me to have the greatest respect and admiration for her.

Still, I longed for a closer relationship with my father. Most of our brief conversations ended in an overwhelming feeling of guilt that I should be doing more to make our relationship work. But I was doing all I knew how to do, and his repeated comments, "You'll never amount to anything," weren't all that encouraging to an impressionable young child.

I inherited my tall, lean build from my father. It gained me admission to the girls' basketball team at my school, but little admiration from Dad. I remember the day that he finally came to watch me play. I was into my seventh year of playing basketball, yet he hadn't attended a single game. Needless to say, I wanted to play my best that night. Unfortunately, I did just the opposite. I fouled out of the game within minutes of his arrival. Dad never bothered to come again, even though I eventually became captain of the team, won numerous awards, and was voted the MVP (Most Valuable Player).

In the years that followed, when I would visit my father he was barely able to carry on a conversation with me for more than an hour. After that, he made it clear that it was time for me to leave. I had become accustomed to his emotional distance, and didn't expect much more, so you can imagine my reaction when, during one of our telephone conversations, he abruptly told me that he loved me. I was nearly fifty years old at the time. I suppose what they say is true—aging tends to soften people.

Until the day he died, I tried to maintain some type of relationship with my father. I felt that I should honor him, as the Bible said I should, but he never made it easy.

When my father died and the curtain closed on any chance for a close relationship with him, it broke my heart. At the funeral, the minister talked about what a wonderful person my father was and shared interesting things that I never even knew about him. At first, anger raged within me to know that I wasn't a part of his life, but then I began to be thankful that I had at least gotten to know my dad a little bit after alcohol had quit controlling his life.

I miss my father, but I missed him when he was alive. Through my experience, though, I've developed a new compassion for others experiencing the pain of broken or distant relationships. I'm able to tell them that God can be the father they never had. I know, because He's been that for me.

Ann Aiken

A Step Toward Healing

Think of a broken relationship in your life. If you had this person's attention for five minutes, what would you say? If he or she had your attention, what do you think this person would want to say?

Do you think there is any common ground on which you both could agree?

If there is no immediate healing in this relationship, what do you think you've learned from your experience that might be of help to you in future relationships?

Chapter 14

A Change of Direction

Being confident of this, that he who began a good work in you will carry it on to completion until the day of Christ Jesus.

PHILIPPIANS 1:6

Wouldn't it be nice if we never made a mistake? If we hit all home runs, and didn't break a single window? If we got straight A's on our report cards, won the national spelling bee, gave a perfect piano recital, and were so competent on our computer it didn't even need a "delete" key?

Unfortunately, we do need that "delete" key from time to time, because we aren't perfect. In fact, we're far from it.

If we were to take a baby boy and a baby girl and give them a nickel for every mistake they made from birth, they'd no doubt be millionaires by the time they were three years old. Mistakes, wrong turns, bad decisions, poor judgment calls— they're a part of our lives from the onset. Ever since we first tried standing on our own, there's not one of us who hasn't stumbled, trying to find our footing. Worse than stumbling, we've spilled things on ourselves, wandered off to places to which we had no business wandering off, and, on occasion, found ourselves in the middle of a mess too big for us to clean up on our own. We did it through our terrible twos, our elementary-school years, and our teens, and we'll probably still be doing it into our fifties, sixties, and beyond. But like the old saying goes, "Don't throw the baby out with the bath water."

No matter how many wrong turns we've made in life, we can still get back on the right path. No matter how many times we've sold ourselves short, we're still priceless in God's eyes. No matter how much dirt gets on us, we can still come clean. Dirt isn't permanent. Neither are mistakes. Sometimes the dirt gets a little hard and it takes a good deal more effort to get rid of it, but it still comes off. Every last bit of it.

So, don't ever be fooled into thinking you've made a mistake from which you can never recover. You can always recover. You can turn around and change your direction. You can give yourself the life you deserve, instead of the one you're settling for. God wants that for you. But you have to want it for yourself, too.

When I was growing up, there was a girl who lived down the street from us. She was the sister of one of my good friends, and by the sixth grade, it became painfully obvious that she was hanging around with the wrong crowd. She got involved in the drug scene, and before long she was on a steady descent, from one drug to the next and the next. Drugs became her life, until one night they took it from her. She overdosed on heroin and died.

I don't believe she intended for her life to end that way. Somewhere along the line she must have had dreams, hopes, and aspirations. But she took a single wrong turn, and instead of realizing that and turning around, she kept on going down that path to nowhere. That one wrong turn became two wrong turns, then three, and before she knew it, she had lost control of her life. She was no longer making the decisions. The drugs were. And even if she had wanted to change, the friends she had surrounded herself with weren't going to let her, because her addiction had become a financial benefit to them.

So she died of an overdose at nineteen years of age.

It's not easy to stand by and watch a friend or family member continually make poor choices, especially when those choices ultimately cost that person his or her life. Even though you may have done your best to intervene, you still feel guilty, wondering if there was something else you could have done to stop the downward spiral.

I've often wondered what it was that got my friend's sister started down the path that would eventually lead to her death. Was it that first experimentation with drugs? Or was it when she started hanging around with the wrong crowd? I say those are only the symptoms. Her problem began long before that. It began when she first started listening to the inner voice that told her, "This is all I'm worth." For some reason, she believed that lie. Once she believed that, the wrong decisions just kept falling into place.

Only God knew and could judge the condition of that girl's heart at the moment of her death. I couldn't. But I do know that He had so much more planned for her life than what she settled for. And even though it's difficult to find any good out of a senseless death like this, if it helps us try just a little harder next time to prevent someone else—even ourselves—from meeting that same fate, then perhaps this death, and others like it, will not have been in vain.

Addiction's a thief
that slyly steals our loved ones
right before our eyes.

                                    Haiku by Diantha Ain

When You're Lonely ...

Sitting in the back seat of the car that night, I could feel the tiny clusters of butterflies in my stomach. The driver of the car was just an acquaintance at the time. Yet I was lonely, and desperate for a friend.

When we arrived at our destination, I felt a calmness, a sense of serenity. I could hear the music and felt my heart racing to keep time with the beat. Someone at the door put a wristband on my arm. I looked around at the room and smiled. I had discovered a new life. It was my first party, my first rave.

Fifteen minutes later I had a pill in one hand and a bottled water in the other. I was told the pill was a mitsu, an ecstasy pill. Without thinking about the consequences, I swallowed it. At first, I didn't notice any effects, but an hour later I was telling complete strangers that I loved them, and I had a feeling of total acceptance. For the first time in a long while, I was happy. Even if it was artificial, my loneliness was gone. Ecstasy became my drug of choice. It was my alcohol, the friend I so desperately needed.

Those at the rave told me that ecstasy wasn't addictive, which in my mind made it even better. I figured I could take it and stop whenever I wanted to. I vowed to myself that I would take it only in moderate dosages. Every two weeks I would buy one pill. But before long it was one every weekend. Then, it was several every weekend. I was quickly becoming dependent on this drug that they had touted as "harmless." I was becoming emotionally dependent and physically addicted.

Late one night, after an argument with my mother, I left my house and met up with one of my new "friends." At three o'clock in the morning we went to a rave together. I had every intention to "roll" that night, but when I got to the party I heard there were no more "freebies." Within fifteen minutes, I had bought one. I spent the next several moments in my pseudo-state of happiness, bragging to anyone who would listen that I had the so-called right connections. This time, though, the effects of the drug were even more prominent. This pill was somehow different from the others, and the intensity overwhelmed me. I started to hyperventilate and eventually lost consciousness. When I woke up the next day, it was like I was dead. I had no emotions whatsoever. I couldn't bring myself to smile, cry, or even be angry. I felt nothing.

Somehow I made my way home and called my sister. That's when I broke. The tears wouldn't stop. I confessed every lie I had ever told to cover up my new life. I told her what I had become involved with, and she helped talk me through it.

I wish I could say that I hung up the telephone and everything was fine from that point on, but addiction doesn't work that way. The "comedown" lasted for two days. They were the worst two days of my life. Thankfully, I've recovered from my wrong turn. Others haven't been so lucky.

It all started with one pill. A pill that led to another and another and ended up costing me a lot more than the $35 price tag that the pusher placed on it. It cost me my family's trust, and it almost cost me my life.

I was lonely. I didn't have any friends. But I found out that friends can be artificial. Happiness can be artificial, too. Life isn't easy. It never will be. But it's a lot easier sober. It's a lot easier with real friends and real happiness. Don't settle for anything less than God's best for your life.

February 9, 2001, was my last ecstasy pill.
Anonymous

But he said to me, "My grace is sufficient for you, for my power is made perfect in weakness."

2 CORINTHIANS 12:9

Life is what we make it, always has been, always will be.
Grandma Moses

When You Encounter Unexpected Turbulence

October 31, 1994. Halloween. A typical fall day in my neighborhood. My costume? An accident victim. After a successful round of trick-or-treating, I carried my stash home and went to bed, savoring one last taste of some freshly acquired chocolate.

Around 4:30 in the morning, I was awakened by my mother's screams. She'd just received news that my dad's plane had gone down somewhere in the Chicago area. Alicia, my older sister, kept reassuring me that Dad was on another plane. Since it was too early to get any useful information, we piled into the station wagon and headed to my grandmother's house in Rockville to wait.

Word finally came. He was indeed on the ill-fated aircraft,

and there were no survivors. Tim Bruce Bramley, my father, was dead at forty-eight years of age.

My mind raced with questions. Why did it happen? Why did it have to be my father who was on that plane? Why not someone else's? There are six billion other people in this world. Why did this tragedy have to happen to my family?

When your favorite television show is interrupted with the news of some tragedy in which people have lost loved ones, it's easy to sympathize with the grieving. For a few moments, at least. The media gives a brief life sketch of the deceased, you listen, then wait for your show to resume so you can move on with your day. But when the tragedy is yours, the deceased someone you love, it's very different. Everything you took for granted before is now cherished, life is precious, and petty arguments seem meaningless.

After my father's death, I managed to muddle my way through the sixth grade and moved on into middle school. I had already begun to lose touch with my friends from elementary school. I was no longer with the "in" crowd; to them I was a stranger, and frankly, I wanted it that way. I was hurting so much, I didn't care what anyone thought of me. My new friends were hardly my mother's first choice, but since she was still having difficulties coping with my father's death herself and had to be hospitalized, I hardly ever saw her.

My new friends, Ann and Caitlin (not their real names), had a darkness that drew me in. For the first time in my life, I was exposed to a side of human culture that I had never known about, a side most people in my world refused to talk about— the world of Satanism, witchcraft, and death.

I made my own Ouija board, and began to practice talking

with the dead. There was the endless fantasy of joining a cult, and thoughts of suicide obsessed me for days. I did attempt it several times, but something always stopped me before it was too late. Self-mutilation was another thought that occupied my mind. I would bang my head on the wall, hit myself, or scratch myself with metal hangers. My entire world was twisting out of control. I hated everyone. As for God? I wasn't even sure if there was one.

But one night, at the end of eighth grade, I found myself on the crossroads between life and death. I had put up so many walls to protect me from more hurt, but that night while sitting next to my window, looking out at the pitch-black sky, my defenses finally collapsed. I hadn't even allowed myself to cry at my father's funeral, but that night on my knees, tears began streaming down my face. I knew that I had created the darkness that had been surrounding me and, on my own, I couldn't find my way back out. But from the moment I allowed God to shine His light into my life, and into my hurt, the darkness went away and suddenly there was hope.

Chloe Bramley

Accept no one's definition of your life; define yourself.
Richard Bach

When You Choose Life

There was a young girl, the baby of the family, who was lost. She began to crave another life, a different life, a life where all the pain would go away, and she felt that in order to have that life, she had to leave the one she had.

Her parents had recently separated, and she, along with her mother and one of her brothers, had moved across the country, away from her father, sister, and another brother. She desperately wanted to go home, back to life as it had been.

The girl tried to overpower her mother in decisions. They would argue, fight, then wouldn't speak for days. All the changes she had been going through were too much for her to handle. She had been in a depression for months, living in a separate world from her brother and her mom, doing everything at night and sleeping all day. She was in the eighth grade, but stopped going to school because of repeated anxiety attacks.

One night the girl finally convinced her mom to send her home, but then family members intervened and encouraged her mother to stand strong and deal with the girl's depression, which was the real issue.

"Why did you tell her to do that?" the girl screamed at her older sister over the telephone one night. "Why don't you want me to be happy?"

But her sister remained steadfast. She knew the girl needed help, not escape.

The next couple of days were disastrous. There were endless arguments with her brother, mostly because he would never leave her alone for fear of what she would do to herself. But even with the constant surveillance, she was determined to end it all.

"I hate my life!" she wrote one night in her journal. "I hate my family. I'm sorry that I am going to do this, but I don't want to feel the way I do anymore. I don't want to hurt anyone anymore."

She dotted her last period, closed her journal, and took what she planned to be her last steps toward the bathroom. She opened the medicine cabinet, eagerly looking for pills. She found a bottle that was prescribed for her mother. She had no idea what kind they were, or what they were capable of doing. She just took them, one by one. Then she found another bottle, and gradually started to take handfuls, while staring blankly at herself in the mirror. She took the last pill, its awful taste remaining in her mouth, then started looking for more. There weren't any.

She joined her brother in the living room and watched television like nothing had happened. But an hour later her stomach began to hurt. She felt sick. With a self-preserving instinct she didn't know she had, she went into the bathroom and began to vomit. Her brother followed and tried to help, holding back her hair. She looked up at him, scared and regretting what she had done. For the first time in a long time, she wanted to live, but was it too late?

"I'm sorry, Joey, I'm sorry," she cried. "Call Eunie, call Dad, call Lonnie. I'm sorry."

She could see the fear and confusion in her brother's eyes. Without knowing for certain what his little sister had done, he called each one of the people who just hours before she had said she hated.

"I'm sorry," she apologized to her brother, Lonnie. "I'm so sorry."

"What did you do?" Lonnie asked.

"I'm sick, Lonnie, I'm sick. I don't feel good."

"What did you do?"

"I took pills."

Joey stayed right by her side as she grabbed her stomach, then threw her head back.

"I can't see. The room's spinning," she said.

Her mind was hazy, like she was in a fog. She started to remember things from her childhood. Visions of playing games with her family played over and over in her head. She remembered all the happy times. Then she reflected on the times of fighting, when things started to fall apart. Her head was spinning out of control.

Her mom came home and Joey told her what had happened. After some convincing, the girl finally agreed to be taken to the emergency room.

"How many pills did you take?" the nurse asked.

Her mother handed the nurse one of the empty bottles that she had found in the trash can.

"Huh?" the girl stammered.

The nurse repeated the question, then...

"I stopped counting," she answered.

The girl's head felt heavy, and was rocking as though it was trying to keep balance on her neck.

"When did you stop counting?" the nurse pressed.

"Thirty-five," she said.

Moments later a tube was being shoved down her throat because of her refusal to swallow it voluntarily. Through the tube, doctors administered what looked like black charcoal into her stomach. The girl glanced over at her mother, then quickly turned away, not wanting to see her mother in pain.

The girl lay on her back, no longer capable of fighting the doctors. She stared straight up at the ceiling, almost lifeless. In the right hand corner of the ceiling, she saw a picture of Jesus on the cross. She focused on it. Could He help her? Could He help someone who had refused all help from others? Could He stop this nightmare, and make her life make sense?

So many thoughts whirled through her head, and at one point she wondered if she were already dead. At long last, however, the tube was taken out and she was out of danger. The doctors told her mother that had she gotten her to the hospital just fifteen minutes later, they probably wouldn't have been able to save her.

That girl was me five years ago. My memories of life back then are just a blur, but that's one night I will never forget. That night not only changed my life, it began my life. It was as if I had been in a slumber, a black hole, and didn't want to or couldn't crawl out of it. When I look in the mirror today, the reflection I see is still the reflection of that thirteen-year-old face. But instead of seeing hopelessness, I see possibilities. Instead of seeing a girl who wants to escape, I see a girl who wants to live, and live life to the fullest.

I am very thankful for what I have now. There has been so much that I have accomplished in the years that followed that night, things that I never would have experienced if I had been successful in my attempt to end my life. I joined my school's journalism team and have been fortunate enough to win twenty-seven student journalism awards, including Broadcast Journalist of the Year for the state of Arkansas.

More importantly, though, I discovered that I'm a winner at life. Regardless of the circumstances in which I find myself, I can, with God's help, overcome them. My parents are still separated, but I know they love me. My family also loves me, and the best change of all is that I love myself.

Most failure in life is looked at negatively, but I'm so very thankful that I failed at my attempt that night and gave myself a second chance at life. Who would have thought that's what I wanted all along? Not death, but life. Not ending it all, but finally starting it all.

Lisa Lopez
Age 18

Hope, like the gleaming taper's light
Adorns and cheers our way;
And still, as darker grows the night,
Emits a brighter ray.

Oliver Goldsmith
The Captivity

When you do nothing, you feel overwhelmed and power-less. But when you get involved, you feel the sense of hope and accomplishment that comes from knowing you are working to make things better.

Pauline R. Kezer

A Step Toward Healing

List what you've learned from a few of the wrong choices you may have made in life.

Do you believe our wrong choices determine our futures, or do you think we determine our futures by the direction in which we head after making a wrong choice?

Chapter 15

Saying Goodbye to Bitterness

I have told you these things, so that in me you may have
peace. In this world you will have trouble. But take
heart! I have overcome the world.

JOHN 16:33

It's easy to get bitter when life treats us unfairly, isn't it? Why
did it have to be us who lost a parent? Why did we have to
watch our brother die, or say goodbye to a grandparent long
before we wanted to? Why did our parents have to get divorced?
Why couldn't this have happened to someone, anyone else? It
just isn't fair!

Though you may not know it yet, unfairness is fertile soil in
which the root of bitterness can grow. When life is unfair, we're
at war within ourselves, alternating between the desire to accept
our trials with grace and wanting to be real and vent our anger
and hurt. Acceptance is healthy, and forgiving those who may
have caused harm to someone we love is, too, but true healing
after a loss won't occur until we've honestly faced our disappointment, hurt, and anger head-on. Pretending those feelings
don't exist will merely delay the healing process. We might be
able to fool others into thinking we're OK, but deep down we
know we have those feelings. God knows we do, too. Perhaps

even our close friends know we do. So for whom are we putting on the brave face? Strangers? People who don't even know us and who couldn't care less how our healing is going?

The sooner we deal with our true emotions, the sooner we can get back to being ourselves again. Admitting hurt or anger over the loss of someone you loved, or the disappointment you're feeling over dashed dreams, doesn't make you any less of a Christian. It makes you human.

So when life is unfair, be honest about its unfairness and the pain it has caused you, get angry if you feel like it, but then, begin to move on with your life as soon as possible. Bitterness will only stunt your growth. When you face your trials and thrive in the midst of them, you go from being a victim to being an overcomer.

God offers lifelines
to all those floundering in
a sea of despair.

Haiku by Diantha Ain

Although the world is full of suffering, it is also full of the overcoming of it.

Helen Keller

When Consistency Counts

The death of my father hit me harder than I thought it would. In view of the fact that he and my mother had gone through a bitter divorce when I was eleven years old. They had married late in life, so I suppose by then they were both a little set in their ways.

To this day, I can still recall the constant fighting and numerous separations. Unfortunately, I was told about every detail of the divorce, numerous times over, by my mother. At eleven, you don't always realize there are two sides to every situation, so my relationship with my dad was strained, to say the least. I remember having to tell the court and my father's attorney which parent I wanted to live with. That's a difficult decision for an eleven-year-old boy, and it's uncomfortable to have to choose between two people you love.

Looking back on it now as an adult, I can certainly see where, yes, my father failed as a husband, and perhaps he wasn't even the best example of fatherhood, but he did have some good qualities that I will always admire. Now that he's gone, I regret not ever having told him that or gotten to know him a little better.

My father was dependable. If he promised to pick me up at five o'clock to go get a hamburger, he would be there at five o'clock sharp. My father was financially responsible, too. Every Friday was payday, and Dad would pick me up and take me with him on his weekly journey around town, paying his bills. He was faithful with his alimony payments, as well. That was never an issue between him and my mother. And he had a high work ethic. He wasn't afraid of hard work, and his attendance record was impeccable. Even when he had all of his teeth removed (a somewhat unorthodox treatment for arthritis that was suggested by his doctor), my father reported to work directly after leaving the oral surgeon's office, cotton padding still in his cheeks. He never forgot to send me a card on my birthday, and even attended my wedding—something my mother couldn't bring herself to do because "he was going to be there."

In most divorces, one side is painted as the "good" and one side is painted as the "bad." Yet, more often than not, neither side is all good or all bad. My mother and father got divorced. Not me and my dad. She no longer loved him, and maybe had every right not to. But I stopped loving a man who really hadn't done anything wrong to me. Sure, I wished he had been more involved in my life, but maybe he didn't feel welcome. Maybe he felt those walls of bitterness that I had allowed to build up between us for no good reason.

The fact that my father was as involved in my life as he was proved that I meant something to him. My mother loved me, there was no doubt of that. But my father loved me, too. He didn't always know how to show it, but his consistency in my life spoke it loud and clear. I just wish I had seen it sooner.

Anonymous

Let him who would enjoy a good future waste none of his present.

Dale Carnegie

When You Have to Forgive

My best friend, Mary (not her real name), and I were inseparable. We'd been friends since the sixth grade, and there wasn't anything we couldn't tell each other. We would talk about guys, fashion, school, everything.

In the seventh grade, though, Mary and another friend began to hang out together. I didn't understand why Mary had quit spending time with me until one day when she confided that her new friend had told her not to be my friend because I use crutches. So, not wanting to lose that friendship, she sacrificed mine and never spoke to me again.

For awhile I became very depressed. I wouldn't eat. All I wanted to do was just sit and cry. This went on for weeks, but eventually I began to put it behind me and move on with my life.

It would be very easy for me to still harbor anger and hatred in my heart toward both of these girls, but I don't. God has helped me to let it go and move on. He has shown me that no matter what someone does to you, you should wish that person blessings and forgive him or her. Yet, God's kind of forgiveness doesn't mean to deny the pain someone has caused you. It means acknowledging both the offense and the offender, but choosing to forgive.

Make no mistake about it, it hurt to find out that my best friend didn't consider my friendship worth standing up for. It hurt to have someone break up a friendship that I had cherished. Yet it's just not worth it to hate. It takes too much energy. It also makes you a bitter person, and you run the risk of it eventually hardening your heart toward God's love. That's a risk I don't want to take. We all need God's love in our lives. I do. Mary does. And though she probably doesn't even realize it, so does Mary's new friend.

Melody Romero
15 years old

You can't be brave if you've only had wonderful things happen to you.

Mary Tyler Moore

A Step Toward Healing

Make a list of the benefits that you expect to get from remaining bitter.

Make a list of the benefits that could come from letting go of bitterness.

Chapter 16

Near Losses

The Lord your God is with you, he is mighty to save. He will take great delight in you, he will quiet you with his love, he will rejoice over you with singing.

ZEPHANIAH 3:17

None of us knows the exact number of years we've been given, but however many it is, God knows the precise amount, down to the minute, and He has a plan for each of us.

I wouldn't ever have made it to my first birthday if God's plan for my life hadn't included more time than that. But it did.

It was Christmas Eve. I was three months old. My family had just left my uncle and aunt's home in Searcy, Arkansas, en route to our own house when we were hit head-on by a drunk driver. Our car was thrown into a ditch and was completely totaled. It's a miracle that any of us made it out alive. My father had the most severe injuries, requiring a lengthy hospital stay and numerous blood transfusions. The rest of us had varying degrees of injuries. My arm was broken, although it wasn't discovered right away. My cousin, Patsy Scott, and her parents, who were watching me while my mother and father were hospitalized, noticed that I cried whenever anyone moved my arm. They took me to a doctor and an X-ray quickly verified what my cousin and her family already knew—I had indeed broken my arm in the car wreck. Since it was my writing hand, I think I might owe them some royalties.

My arm healed and I continued on with my life. I've had numerous close calls since, but God's purpose for my existence isn't over yet, so I keep plugging along. The fact that you're reading this book means God's plan for your life isn't over yet, either. In fact, as long as you have breath, you can be assured that you still have a purpose to fulfill in your life. The loved ones to whom we've had to say goodbye apparently have fulfilled their purposes. They may still be fulfilling those purposes even after their death, but their work here on earth is done. Ours isn't.

When Lauren Hutton broke both her legs and arms, as well as crushing three ribs and puncturing a lung in a motorcycle accident, it didn't appear she was going to pull through. Yet the actress and supermodel credits a series of "miracles" with saving her life.

On *Good Morning America*, Lauren told Diane Sawyer that moments before the accident, fellow rider Jeremy Irons insisted she change her helmet to one with a visor, and earlier that day, friend Dennis Hopper had insisted she wear a heavier leather jacket than what she had planned on wearing. These acts, said Lauren, no doubt saved her life. The tires on Lauren's motorcycle lost their grip on a curve and she skidded some 100 feet before becoming airborne, hitting the ground, and skidding another 170 feet—this time on her face. Lauren was right—had it not been for the visor and the jacket, she never would have survived.

Lauren realizes she's been blessed with another chance at life and she's determined to make it count. "I really feel like this is all extra time, you know?" she told Diane Sawyer. "I just got extra time."

So, appreciate every day that you've been blessed with, and get busy accomplishing those things that God has planned for you to accomplish. The clock is ticking. Don't waste a moment of your life.

Even though I walk through the valley of the shadow of death, I will fear no evil, for you are with me; your rod and your staff, they comfort me.

PSALM 23:4

There's strength in numbers,
which must be why prayer chains
create miracles.

Haiku by Diantha Ain

When a Close Call Brings You Closer

On the night my family and I were celebrating my fifteenth birthday, we learned that my oldest sister had just discovered a lump near her breast. She told us about all the tests they were performing to determine the seriousness of the lump.

We prayed as a family, and continued to pray for the next several days until the phone call came, telling my mother that the lump was indeed malignant. My sister had breast cancer.

I was at my friend's house when my mother called to tell me the news. I remember hanging up the phone and just standing there in my friend's room, in shock at what I had just been told.

I shared the situation with my friend, but she didn't really know what to say. Most people don't know what to say at times like this. They think they have to say something brilliant, and if they can't, they don't say anything. I didn't need brilliance. I just needed a friend to listen.

I walked the few blocks back to my home. When my mother opened the door, we hugged and cried for a long time. Then my dad started crying. In my entire life I had never seen my father cry. There was so much uncertainty, and there were so many questions, so many prayers to pray.

My sister selected her course of treatment and the fight for her life began. All we could do was put our trust in God and believe that He had everything under control. My sister was going for her master's degree in art history when she was stricken with the disease. After her treatments started, her hair fell out, she was sick a lot, and she seemed to grow weaker each time I saw her. Yet she never gave up. None of us ever gave up.

Thank God we didn't. Today, her hair is back and the cancer is gone. Completely. She received her master's degree and is now teaching at various colleges in our area. As for the rest of us? We'll never forget this chapter of our lives. We're so thankful to have our sister back. And to have a God who can heal, and does.

Lisa Miceli
Age 19

The world is round, and the place which may seem like the end may also be the beginning.

Ivy Baker Priest

For you have delivered me from death and my feet from stumbling, that I may walk before God in the light of life.

PSALM 56:13

When You Have Doubts

I was brought up in a Christian home, but recently I went through a low period in my life. I wanted to believe, but I just couldn't without evidence.

Then, one night, as I was attending a youth bonfire and fireworks display, the fireworks started to misfire, trapping six of us in their path and hitting one of my friends. I was so scared. Whatever doubts I had about God before that night sure left in a hurry as I called out to Him to save us. He answered my prayer as our youth leader ran across the field to us, then covered us with his body, protecting us from the raining fireworks.

I know now that I need God each and every day of my life. No doubt about it.

Ruth Risbridger
Age 15

Adversity makes men think of God.

Livy

A Step Toward Healing

Think of a near loss you've had recently. What did the experience teach you about the fragility of life?

In what ways do you think you've changed since this near loss?

Chapter 17

When a Friend Gives Up

May your unfailing love be my comfort, according to your promise to your servant.

PSALM 119:76

I was in a church service once where the pastor asked for anyone who needed prayer to come forward to the altar. Two of those who answered the invitation formed an impression on me that I'll never forget. One was a young man who had been battling cancer. He was in his twenties and had already lost a leg to the disease. Doctors had given him only a few months to live. The pastor prayed for him, then moved on to the next man in line. This man was healthy and strong, probably in his thirties or forties. When asked for his prayer request, he shared that he had been battling thoughts of suicide. The contrast between these two men was ironic and sad. Here was a young man fighting for his life with everything he had in him standing next to a man who wanted to throw his life away. Life can certainly be ironic at times.

Suicide is never an answer to problems, nor is it a way to get someone to notice your pain. All it does is silence the cry inside you that deserves to be heard, and it creates a lifetime of problems for loved ones left behind. Yes, whether you believe it or not, your cry deserves to be heard. And even if your depression is telling you that people don't care, they do. But they can't help you or show you how much you mean to them if you don't do your part and let them know you're hurting.

My cousin, Lynn, was my best friend, growing up. We did everything together. She'd spend weekends at my house, or I'd spend them at hers. She was my closest confidante, a tremendous encourager of my writing, and she was the best laugher a would-be comedy writer could ever have. We would often stay up late into the night telling jokes or reliving some humorous prank we had played on someone.

I began writing poetry when I was twelve years old, and would tape each poem to the wall above my bed (it was cheaper than wallpaper). Whenever Lynn would come over, she'd scan the wall of poems, looking for any new ones, and I could always count on her to laugh out loud at the funny ones. Hearing her laughter assured me that I was doing something right.

One day, when Lynn and I were both fourteen years old, my mother and sisters picked me up from school. This was a little out of the ordinary, since my mother worked full time and we usually walked home, but not totally out of the question, so I didn't immediately suspect anything was wrong.

We drove for awhile, just making small talk, then my mother tried to find the words to tell me what she needed to say. Finally, my sister just said it: "Lynn's dead."

I don't think I'll ever forget the sound of those words.

"What?!" I gasped, hoping I hadn't heard her correctly.

My mother and sister filled in the details, how Lynn had swallowed some pills the night before. All I could think to do was to get out of the car and run as far away as I could. I didn't know where I would go, nor did I care. I just wanted to run. Run away from the reality of what they were telling me. Run back in time, back to before I had gotten into the car that afternoon.

The next few days were a blur. I couldn't believe she was gone. None of us could. To this day, no one really knows for certain whether Lynn took the pills with the intention of actually ending her life. The fact remains, though, that a beautiful life ended that night. A life full of promise. A life that was loved by all who knew her. Decades later, I still catch myself thinking of Lynn, especially whenever I write a funny poem or a joke. I can almost hear her hearty laugh of approval. Even though she was a part of my life for only fourteen years, I know I'll never forget my cousin and best friend, and I thank God for blessing me with her. My life has been enriched by her presence, her endless encouragement, and especially her laughter. I don't know why she viewed her situation as hopeless that night, or why she forgot how loved she was, and especially, how to laugh. But she did. And if she dropped any hints, I certainly didn't pick up on them.

Do you know someone who may be screaming out to be heard, even though he or she may not be saying a word? Do you, yourself, need to be heard? According to Online Psych, Inc. in 1999, the most commonly cited symptoms of suicide are:

—extreme changes in behavior
—a previous suicide attempt
—a suicidal threat or statement
—signs of depression

If you or anyone you know is exhibiting any of the above

symptoms, please talk with your minister, your parents, or a teacher, or call one of the hotlines listed at the back of this book. No matter how bad things look at the moment, remember there is hope. There is always hope. And there's help—lots of help—just a phone call away.

Suicide doesn't have to be one of the leading causes of death among teens. We can do something to stop it. We can be friends to those around us who feel lonely and overwhelmed. We can listen, and listen some more. We can offer hope. And we can ask for help when we can no longer help ourselves.

When They Don't Share Their Pain

Joey was the class clown, always making everyone laugh. I'd known him since we were in kindergarten. My older brothers were friends of his, and when I first met Joey that September day, I came home from school and told my family I was going to marry him.

During a brief period Joey was home schooled, so I didn't get to see him as much. But he eventually came back to our school, and by the seventh grade he was in my homeroom, which meant we got to see each other every day, all day.

We didn't talk much; often it was just a quick "hey" or a nod as we passed each other in the hall, but I still considered Joey a good friend.

Joey was always doing unpredictable things, like dyeing his hair, so when he came in on May 11, 2000, with a new color, none of us thought much about it. The only thing unusual that day was that he ate lunch by himself, which seemed pretty odd since he was a popular guy and never ate alone.

The next morning when the teacher took attendance in homeroom and we discovered that Joey was absent, we still didn't think anything was seriously wrong. We went through gym class and started Bible class, but then our principal came in and told us we were going to have a meeting. Normally, we would have figured they were just going to tell us about some upcoming activity, but when we saw all the principals there, the headmaster, and a couples' pastor, we began to wonder what was up.

The headmaster opened in prayer, then delivered the tragic news—Joey had taken his own life. The headmaster continued talking, but I have no idea what he said. I couldn't get past the words, "Joey is dead."

I remember going outside and sitting for hours, remembering Joey and crying. We all did a lot of that during the next few days. My brother came over from the high school and held me for what seemed like hours. All the memories of Joey from over the years kept going through my head. I couldn't believe he was gone. How could it be true? It was too horrible to be true.

Our school gave us the day off so those close to Joey could attend his memorial service. The church was packed. I sat near the back with some of my friends, a couple of whom had known Joey for as long as I had. It was a beautiful service. Friends and family shared their memories of Joey. His pastor talked for awhile, but I don't remember much of what he said. One thing I do remember, though, is how he explained that Joey was in a much better place now. You see, Joey was a Christian, a Christian who had obviously suffered from deep depression, even though none of us saw the symptoms. I truly believe Joey is with his Lord now, and those of us he left behind have found some comfort in the memories we carry in our hearts, but we still can't help feeling some guilt, wondering if we could have intervened and done something, anything to have prevented this tragedy. Severe depression can be curable with proper treatment.

We've all learned a valuable lesson in all of this. We've learned to be more aware of others' pain, and to recognize the symptoms of depression. We've also learned to reach out more quickly and offer encouragement and God's love to those around us who may be hurting, because we might be the only one offering it.

Sarah J. Romeo

Believe that life is worth living and your belief will help create the fact.

Oliver Wendell Holmes

Hope never abandons you; you abandon it.

George Weinberg

When Sunny Skies Turn to Gray

It was a warm spring Saturday morning. I had gotten up early so I could do my homework. I tried to concentrate on my work, but all I could think about was the upcoming summer. It had been a long winter, and finally I was going to get to wear short sleeves and shorts!

My summery thoughts were soon interrupted by a telephone call. It was one of my best friends, and grateful for the homework break, I started to talk to her about the new modeling job she might get for that summer. It wasn't long before she shared with me the purpose of her phone call.

Speaking in a low and deliberate voice, she said, "Whitney, I have bad news." I figured she was going to say that she and her boyfriend had broken up yet again. But it was worse, and there was no way I could have prepared myself for it.

"My brother killed himself!" she said, trying to fight back the tears. After a few seconds of stunned silence, all I could manage to say was "I'm so sorry."

What had begun as a beautiful sunny day turned into a emotional downpour in a matter of seconds. Her brother was only twenty-three years old. Why had he given up?

The same night that I received the terrible news, I went to the viewing of the body. The fact that he was gone didn't really sink in until I saw him there that night. A chill went down my spine as I remembered all the times I could have told him about Jesus, and the hope to be found in Him, but didn't.

When I walked over to my friend, she gave me a hug and then whispered in my ear, "I didn't think you would come!" I'm not sure why none of her other friends came, but seeing the look on her face when we hugged, I'm so glad I did.

Even though my friend and I don't go to school together anymore, we're still close. Because I was there for her at her brother's funeral, it took our relationship to a whole new level. It showed her I cared, really cared, and not just with lip service.

I still don't know why her brother felt so hopeless that he decided to take his own life, but I do know that with God's help, I can continue to show his family the hope that can be found only in God.

Whitney Fritts
Age 13

A faithful friend is a strong defense; and he that hath found him hath found a treasure.

Louisa May Alcott

A Step Toward Healing

Why do you think some teens today don't seem to have hope?

If you could talk to them right now, what would you say?

Where are you placing your hope?

*If you have lost someone through suicide, or have had thoughts of suicide yourself, talk with a minister, a youth pastor, your parents, a teacher, or another responsible adult. There are also hotline numbers at the back of this book where you can find help and encouragement.

Chapter 18

Saying Goodbye to Regrets and Wasted Time

The Lord turn his face toward you and give you peace.

NUMBERS 6:26

Life can change in an instant. I remember the night I stood at the foot of the ambulance gurney as the emergency room physician examined our son, Russ.

"Mom!" he cried out in a panic, "Mom!"

I answered, reassuring him that I was there, even though he couldn't see me. The part of Russ' brain where the hematoma had occurred was the part that controlled his vision. He was now blind. Russ was fifteen years old. He had been a part of our family ever since we had adopted him at three weeks of age. He was a special gift from God. And now, all I could do was pray as he lay there sightless and fighting for his life.

The hospital chaplain tried his best to comfort us and offer hope, but as we were later to discover, it had been barely a week since he had witnessed another young man's skateboard injury result in death. He didn't have a lot of hope.

A neurosurgeon from a neighboring city was called in to examine Russ and remained at the hospital on standby throughout the night in the event Russ had additional internal bleeding from the head trauma. If that were to occur, emergency surgery would need to be performed to relieve the mounting pressure on the brain. As for whether Russ' vision would eventually return, no one could say for sure. Right now, they were more concerned with saving his life.

They transferred Russ from the ER to the Intensive Care Unit. The next two days would be critical, they told us. My husband, our other two sons, close friends, and several other family members waited in a special waiting room only a few feet from the ICU door. We were allowed to visit Russ for only a few minutes every hour.

I called every pastor I could think of and asked them to pray. I called churches from the yellow pages, prayer chains, prayer hotlines, and every friend I knew who knew how to pray. I went through a lot of quarters at the pay phone, but I was desperate. Russ' life was hanging in the balance, every minute counted, and prayer was the only answer.

It's strange how your whole world can change in a moment's time, isn't it? When I woke up that morning, I had no idea that I would find myself in an emergency room faced with the very real possibility of losing a son. Life, health, relationships, and happiness can never be taken for granted.

Needless to say, time passed slowly those next few days. But thank God, it also passed uneventfully. There wasn't any additional bleeding in Russ' brain, and his vision did eventually return. After a few more days in ICU, he was moved to a regular room, and later allowed to go home.

It was a close call. Too close. But it reminded us all of how unpredictable life can be. In a single moment your whole world can change. I was with Russ before he went out to play that afternoon. I never dreamed he would be in an ambulance, only a short time later.

So, don't wait until later to do the things you want to do for someone, or say the things you want to say. Live your life so you have no regrets. Don't wait for "someday" to tell someone how much he or she means to you. Make each moment count, because life changes. It changes over time, but it can also change in a moment. And when it does, you may not have another chance to say it.

When All You Have Are Questions

It was a seemingly uneventful, cold winter day in Illinois. I had been walking around the mall with my friend, Elaine, searching for bargains and having some quality "girl time" before wrapping up the weekend. As we stopped to pick up a bite to eat, a childhood companion came up behind me and tapped me on the shoulder.

Mark and I had grown up together, and when I turned and looked into his eyes, I could see that something was terribly wrong. It was, and he wasted no time with formal greetings.

"Christan, have you heard?"

I searched his face for any hint of what was to come, but nothing could prepare me for what I was about to hear.

"It's Matt, Christan. He's ... dead. He overdosed on heroin last night."

Matt? I went numb. Like Mark, Matt was also someone with whom I had grown up. We had played together and ridden the bus to school together, and we had practically lived at each other's houses.

Matt had started experimenting with alcohol, sex, and drugs

at an early age. I had watched him go from marijuana to other hard drugs, including LSD and heroin, the drug that ultimately took his life. Yet, not wanting to upset our friendship, I was afraid to say anything. Before the age of sixteen it never dawned on me to intervene. I simply lived by the rule that life was painful for all of us, and anything we wanted to do to ease that pain was acceptable. After all, they're our lives, right? Besides, I had been doing some experimenting with alcohol and drugs myself until a wonderful young woman named Robin intervened and introduced me to Jesus Christ.

My life changed dramatically after that. I didn't want to do the same things or hang with the same people. I did, though, continue to wonder about Matt. I wondered how he was doing and if he had heard about this Jesus I had come to know and love. I wondered, but whenever I would run into him around town, our friendly but superficial conversations only proved what I already knew—we were growing apart. Matt was still into the drug scene, and I was into the "religious" scene, as he called it. On several occasions I felt God leading me to tell Matt about the new life I had been given ... but I never did.

Weeks after the funeral I became extremely sad, and slipped into a time of deep depression. I didn't want to eat, work, or do anything but sleep. I slept until the last possible moment in the morning, went to school and slept through classes, then came home and slept some more. It was more than the pain of losing a close friend that drove me to this. It was the realization that Matt might have died without knowing Jesus. This loss, this emptiness in my life started to consume my thoughts. I felt responsible, I felt like I had let him down, but more than that, I felt as though I had let God down.

It was during this time of weakness, this time when I was too confused to question anymore and too emotionally spent to cry more tears, that I finally heard the gentle, loving voice of God. He had been there all along, wanting to comfort me so much sooner, but I had been too busy listening to my own pain to hear His reassurance. The words that were spoken to me by Robin, the woman who had led me to Christ, came to mind:

"It's not in running, but in resting; it's not in walking, but in waiting; and it's not in wondering, but in praying that we find the strength of the Lord."

Many people have asked me since then how I finally managed to get over Matt's death. The answer is, I haven't. Not totally. I still struggle with the loss. But whenever it gets to be too much, I surrender my questions to a loving God, and that's when I hear Him say, "I understand, my child. I'll carry the pain from here."

Christan McCoy

I have always grown from my problems and challenges, from the things that don't work out—that's when I've really learned.

Carol Burnett

Treasure each other in the recognition that we do not know how long we shall have each other.

Joshua Loth Liebman

When You Wish It Had Been You

Mary Ann was closer to my age than any of my other siblings, although as a young girl she spent most of her time playing with girls and I with boys.

We had just started to get close about a year before she died. We had begun sharing feelings that we had about people, school, and ourselves. We were becoming real "buddies."

Mary Ann was of medium build, with naturally curly auburn hair and lots of freckles. One of my best friends had a crush on her, so Mary Ann would daily drill me with questions: "Did he say anything about me? Does he like me?" All the typical inquiries. I suppose that's one of the reasons we were drawing closer together. Brothers can provide a wealth of information in situations like these.

Another reason might have been that God knew how very short Mary Ann's life here on earth was going to be.

I was with Mary Ann the day she drowned. A group of us were floating on an automobile inner tube in a reservoir near our home when it capsized, dumping us into the deep, cold water. We tried swimming to safety, but not all of us made it. I managed to save one girl who was with us that day, but I wasn't able to save my sister. At the most crucial moment, Mary Ann's hand was just out of reach.

Since that day, I've carried a lot of mixed feelings over the incident, and a lot of unanswered questions. I've asked God over and over why I didn't drown instead of Mary Ann. She was so full of life, and although she wasn't one of the most popular girls at school, you couldn't find anyone who didn't like her.

I hid when friends and relatives from our church came by the house after the wake. I hid because I felt ashamed, ashamed that I hadn't died instead of her. It wasn't until years later that I realized that God, in all His wisdom, knew I wasn't ready to go that day. My work wasn't done yet. Mary Ann's was.

After my sister's death, I remember having a dream about her. It was as though she were alive again, and I was excited when I woke up. I wanted to tell her about it, so I ran into the girls' bedroom and called out, "Mary!" I stopped short when I saw her empty bed and remembered she wasn't with us any more. I began to cry uncontrollably. I remembered crying some at the lake when we were trying to find her body, and then later when we did find it and were trying to resuscitate her, but that morning after the dream was my first total release of emotions. It was that morning that I truly began the healing process.

One of the most difficult things for me was going to school after the tragedy. It seemed as if everyone wanted me to relive every single detail of what had happened. I was thankful when one of the school's football stars yelled at the crowd that was forming and told them to have some respect and leave me alone. Surprisingly, they did.

I've thought about Mary Ann often throughout the years, and as a teen, I frequently visited her grave. On my graduation day, I visualized what she would have looked like in a cap and gown. Years later, when I was in Vietnam, I sent my mother money and asked her to plant roses at the head of Mary Ann's grave. I even still have a lock of Mary Ann's hair that I found on the floor where she had cut it just before she died.

We probably never really get over the loss of someone we love. We learn to cope, to go on, to trust that God has us in His care and in His plan. And although I wish Mary Ann could still be here with me, good has come from the tragedy because I have now totally committed my life to the Lord. I look forward to seeing my sister again someday in heaven. Until then, I have my memories.

Ernie Stevens

Now is your time of grief, but I will see you again and you will rejoice, and no one will take away your joy.

JOHN 16:22

A Step Toward Healing

All of us could go through life dwelling on our regrets. Why do you think that isn't what God would want us to do?

If you're having a difficult time forgiving yourself for something you did or didn't do for someone, or perhaps even couldn't do for someone, but you still feel guilty, write a letter to that person (even if he or she is no longer here) and share what's on your heart. Once you've written the letter, you can save it or discard it.

Chapter 19

Saying Goodbye to Fear and Hopelessness

> For I am convinced that neither death nor life, neither angels nor demons, neither the present nor the future, nor any powers, neither height nor depth, nor anything else in all creation, will be able to separate us from the love of God that is in Christ Jesus our Lord.
>
> ROMANS 8:38,39

Throughout our lives we may have feelings of fear and hopelessness. These feelings will often follow a period of loss.

It's easy to forget that these feelings are temporary. Your situation may look bleak at the moment. You may not be receiving a single word of encouragement from anybody, not even your church friends. You might be so afraid that you hardly recognize yourself. But don't let anything take your eyes off the Author of Hope and His promises for you. God tells us in the Bible that "nothing is impossible for Him." He's not limited to what your friends, your youth pastor, your relatives, or anyone else believes He can do. He can do anything ... period. His power exists whether we believe in it or not, and thankfully, it isn't limited to our doubts.

Sometimes, though, the answers to our prayers come in a

way we don't expect. We pray for our dad to be healed, but he passes away instead. We pray for our sister to beat that cancer, but she doesn't. At times like that, we simply have to trust in His will. The fact that these people weren't healed here on earth doesn't mean that God doesn't have the power to do it. It just means He had a different plan.

My sister Linda was the eldest girl in our family of one boy and four girls. I was the youngest of the group, and I wasn't even born yet when Linda first developed diabetes at the age of four. All of my memories of Linda included her having the disease.

Growing up, all I really knew about diabetes was that Linda had to have an injection of insulin every day. Sometimes, several injections. I remember walking to the pharmacy down the street to buy her insulin supplies, and to this day I can vividly recall all the times I rounded the corner coming home from elementary school only to find an ambulance parked in front of our house. I'd race home and discover my sister had suffered yet another severe low blood sugar reaction and was now convulsing on the living room floor. The emergency workers were always able to bring her around with intravenous glucose, but the memory of those scenes still make my heart race whenever I hear the wail of an ambulance siren.

In recent years, diabetes treatment has made remarkable advances. While it remains a serious disease, the advanced equipment and new knowledge in treating diabetes has made it far more manageable than it was when my sister was coping with it. When I, myself, became diabetic at eighteen years of age, many of these advances had already become routine in diabetic care.

Yet Linda had to deal with the disease back when the prognosis was far less promising. When she was first diagnosed at four, her condition was so serious that doctors told my parents she might not live. But she did. In her teens, she came close to death several more times. She married in her twenties, and was later told she couldn't have a baby and survive. She had a baby and lived. In her thirties, she had several more close calls. Linda came through each one of them, to the surprise of all of us. In spite of the complications that can sometimes come with diabetes (and eventually she did have several of them), Linda was blessed with well over forty years of living with the disease.

So don't ever give up hope for a loved one, for yourself, or for society. Even when things look bleak, even when doctors tell you there is no hope, even when the unthinkable happens, there's still hope. Time and time again, they told my sister there was no hope, but time and time again she proved them wrong. Each one of us is living on God's time clock, not man's. When it's our time to go, then we'll go on home. Not a day before.

Your life has a purpose. There's a reason you're here for the time that you're here. Live like you know it.

When Someone Forgets His Worth

Kevin (not his real name) has been in trouble with the police and school officials since he was thirteen years old. Today, at nineteen, he is locked down in a 10' x 10' brick room with a metal toilet, a metal sink, and an army cot. Kevin was driving a car during a crime and ran over one of his best friends and another young man in his hurry to get away from the scene.

This handsome young man will now be in prison until he's nearly forty years old.

On the day I met Kevin, he had been involved in a fight with one of the other inmates and now both men were in isolation. Isolation meant they got out of their rooms for only one hour a day and could go "outside" (weather permitting) only into a 10' x 10' fenced-in box.

As Kevin shared his story with me, his bitterness seemed to fill the room.

"I've ruined my life several times over," he said, looking down at the dark gray floor of his cell. "I don't care if I get hurt and I don't care if I hurt someone else. But," he added, "my girlfriend, who's a Christian and has never done anything wrong, brought a little bag of dope into the visiting room for me." It took him nearly a minute to compose himself before continuing. "I talked her into it and the dogs sniffed it out. Now she's facing a one-year mandatory sentence for possession and conspiracy to distribute narcotics. I'm so ashamed. Not only have I ruined my life, but now I've ruined hers. Do you think God can forgive me?"

The bars on Kevin's cell weren't the only ones that were keeping him incarcerated. He had built his own bars out of self-hate, shame, and substance abuse.

"Of course God can forgive you," I tried to encourage him. Yet believing that was going to be the easy part for Kevin. The hard part for Kevin would be forgiving and loving himself.

Tears fell down onto my hands as I held Kevin's through the iron bars. It hit me pretty hard that this young man, like so many of us, had squandered the inheritance God gave him, for little in exchange.

By refusing to acknowledge the price tag God's placed on our lives, we're destined to continually sell ourselves short. Each one of us has worth. God looks beyond our failures and sees our potential. Even when we're covered with dust and rust and whatever else we've allowed to attach itself to our lives, each of us is valuable to Him.

Even Kevin.

Joey Gautier
Comedian

Our part is the trusting, it is God's part to accomplish the results.

Hannah Whitall Smith

When Everything Changes in an Instant

It was a sunny Thursday afternoon in February and I wasn't in the best of moods since I'd had to stay at school until 5:30 for the dress rehearsal of our musical, *Annie*. It hadn't gone well (like most rehearsals), so when my parents picked me up all I could do was complain about how exhausted I was. I still had homework to finish and projects to type, but that didn't seem to matter. My mother and father were insistent on taking my two older brothers and me out to eat. I was hungry, so I didn't rebel too much, but then my dad called a "Family Meeting" when we got home (which I figured meant he had found the spot where I'd spilled spaghetti). Needless to say, I wasn't very excited.

Then the storm came: My parents told us that the stomach

cramps Dad had been having for the past month were the symptoms of a softball-sized tumor in his abdomen. The cancer was called lymphoma, which is a very slow-growing and often curable type of cancer. I have held onto that hopeful word "curable" ever since that night.

I remember the first feelings I had when I learned of my dad's cancer. They were feelings of loss, confusion, anger, and fear of impending change. I couldn't comprehend why God would bring something so incredibly life-altering our way when I was pretty happy and satisfied with how everything was going just then. But then God reminded me of the scripture, "Do not be anxious about anything, but in everything, by prayer and petition, with thanksgiving, present your requests to God. And the peace of God which transcends all understanding will guard your hearts and your minds in Christ Jesus." Even though I had no idea how to handle all the painful feelings that were quickly filling my heart, I gathered them up and gave them over to God, recognizing that He was in control and that His plan for my life was perfect.

It also helped to remember the words one of my closest friends told me: "Always stay in God's hand. Even if you're kickin' and screamin', you're still there, in His control. When you finally give up and surrender to Him, you'll be resting in the peace of His hand."

Now, whenever I'm upset, confused, or hurt, or when something unforeseen happens, I simply say to myself, "I am in God's hand." The road may be rocky, winding, and even impossible at times, but Jesus has carried me all the way so far, and I know He won't let me go now. His nail-scarred hand is a constant hiding place of comfort, and for me, it will always be a special haven where hurts and confusion fade away.

And now there is good news to report! My dad just had a CAT scan and doctors couldn't find any trace of the cancer! The tumor is totally gone. He was supposed to go through another four months of treatment, but now there's no need!

I can't say why my father had to have cancer in the first place or why our family had to go through this crisis, but I do know this—because of Dad's cancer our family has a deeper understanding of the goodness of God. We now know we can trust Him, and when life gets too turbulent, we know our way to that "safe haven"—we head straight for His arms.

Jessica Graham
Age 14

I'm not afraid of storms, for I am learning to sail my ship.

Louisa May Alcott

Saying Good-Bye to So Many

Tuesday morning, September 11, 2001. The month and day: 9-11. A morning that changed the world forever, and a morning that millions of fellow New Yorkers and I will never forget. Nor will any American. Nor will the world.

When I called a friend that morning, he told me to turn on my television. I did, and what soon came into view was the unbelievable, the unimaginable. On virtually every network, a nightmare was unfolding before our nation that would soon test the resolve of even the most seasoned newscaster. Terrorists had attacked America. By using hijacked commercial airlines, they had crashed into the World Trade Towers and the Pentagon, and in the process took thousands of innocent men, women, and children from their families.

I live on 181st Street near Broadway, maybe ten miles away from the World Trade Center. I often ride the subway that goes directly underneath it. In fact, I used to work in the World Trade Towers area. This was a direct hit into America's heart, and a direct hit into mine, as I have many friends who still work down there.

As I watched the horrifying images come across my screen, I knew I had to try to do something to help. So I left my apartment and walked downtown toward the scene of the devastation. This is my account of what I saw and how I felt that day, and in the days that followed:

Not a cloud in the sky except for the billows of smoke pouring out from what used to be the World Trade Center.

A Stealth Fighter flies overhead. Not something we see everyday here in New York City.

People on the streets in my neighborhood standing on the sidewalk, bewildered, numb, nervously talking nonstop. Others praying silently as many churches have opened their doors.

Cops everywhere.

Traffic backed up in front of my building, and as far as I can see down the block. An endless concert of ear-piercing emergency response sirens.

Lines of desperate people wrapped around the block, trying to exit the area by way of the George Washington Bridge, the only bridge still open. People jumping into the back of pickup trucks and other open vehicles in order to exit the city.

Grocery store shelves emptying before my eyes as panicked people try to do something to regain some sense of security. Within hours, maybe minutes, there is no bread left on the shelves.

No traffic on the West Side Highway. Everything normal and routine has come to a halt.

News reports of people jumping to their death from the burning World Trade Center make me cry.

Sadness hangs heavy in the air, both outside and inside where I used to feel so safe.

My friend, Amy, stays overnight at my apartment that night. Amy lives downtown and doesn't want to be alone. Neither do I. No one does.

The next day another friend, Aimee, her baby, and I all make our way down Lexington Avenue to the Armory where the city has organized hopeful people looking for missing loved ones. Family members are everywhere, still in shock, with pictures taped to their chests or clutched in their hands, crowding the streets in endless lines. Even the sweltering heat hasn't deterred them. The media is blocked off across the street, forbidden to approach the grief-stricken throng.

We sign a volunteer list, talk to some media people and others in the area, and give socks to the Salvation Army truck.

Fire stations have been turned into memorials. We grieve silently and look at large posters of the men lost, surrounded by flowers. There are people crowded around just standing and staring. Cookies and cakes are handed out to all who pass by.

We walk on, toward Union Square Park, where hundreds have gathered with their handmade posters bearing the names of their loved ones. Important information is included on each poster, such as height, weight, race, and their last known location in the World Trade Center. Some even include the last words spoken by the missing. A shrine was made with a piece of the WTC. It is surrounded by notes, flowers and candles. The scene is riveting and tragic. So very tragic.

I feel helpless. Helpless to do anything significant enough in a world gone so mad. And I feel guilty. Guilty to continue living my little life when someone, anyone, might be still alive under all the debris.

But sadly, no one is.

Today, as I write this one week after the devastation, rescue workers are having to deal with the painful reality that no one else who was in or around the buildings that day has survived this tragedy. It's the final cruel blow to a heartless, senseless act. Every time I see a poster or sign (and they are everywhere) with a missing face and name, I feel the need to stop, mourn, and give respect. It is overwhelming. How can I grieve the loss of thousands of lives? My heart aches.

They tell us to get back to living. To go about our routine as much as possible.

And I try. I really try. But I feel so guilty. I'm not alone in that feeling here or around America. So much has changed. The Manhattan skyline that I love so much has changed forever. I have changed. My friends have changed. Our leaders have changed. Even our heroes have changed. They're no longer the ones who have sunk the most baskets or recorded the hottest music video. Now, they're airline passengers who have sacrificed their own lives to bravely prevent another tragedy from befalling one of America's great landmarks, they're hundreds of firefighters and police officers who lost their lives while running up the stairs of a burning building to save others, and they're a sea of volunteers—construction workers, blood donors, Red Cross workers, the Salvation Army, counselors, politicians, and companies and individuals who did what they could to help others, even in the midst of their own pain and exhaustion.

America has changed, too. We no longer take our freedoms for granted. And we've once again returned to our knees. For decades, we have pushed God out of our schools, separated church and state, fought to remove His name from our dollar and now ... NOW we turn to Him. Why? Because He is constant. He is love. He is peace. He is joy. He is the foundation this country was founded on, like it or not. And He does not falter. God isn't responsible for the evil of the September 11th tragedy. Terrorists are. But God wants us to know that in the midst of our pain, in the midst of our fears, His arms are ever open, ever ready for us to run into them. He is the almighty Comforter. He is our friend.

A lot of people had to say goodbye to loved ones on September 11, 2001.

My friend, Ralph Murphy, of the New York Police Department, lost half his unit, and so did his brother who is a firefighter. He said the screams of his men on the police radio will haunt him forever.

None of us will ever understand the why of such a tragic event. It's impossible to get inside the mind of anyone who would plan, finance, and execute such a ruthless, barbaric act against innocent human life. But I do not fear. Instead, I take comfort in knowing that God cares, God knows suffering (from the cross), God hears our prayers, and He can, and already has in so many ways, turned this evil around for good. No matter what, God is still very much in charge. And He will reign forever and ever.

Donna East
Comedian

A Step Toward Healing

When your world shatters, where do you find your hope?

Why do you think you can trust God with your future?

Chapter 20

Cherished Memories

I, even I, am he who comforts you.

ISAIAH 51:12

It may be difficult right now to think about your loss without crying. The wound may be too fresh and too deep. But one day, you're going to recall a fun memory of your loved one, and to your surprise, you'll discover the loss hurts just a little bit less. Fond memories are a salve to the spirit. They may sting a little at first, but ultimately they'll aid in your healing process.

When my father died, fond memories of him are what helped me the most. My dad had a great sense of humor. I remember his laughter filling the house as he watched television sitcoms or enjoyed the various antics of such comedians as Red Skelton, Bob Hope, and Jackie Gleason. He loved them all, but had a special fondness for Gleason. I think in some way he might have identified with him.

Like Jackie Gleason, Dad would get into his own predicaments that, in the retelling of them, would bring eruptions of laughter from the family. Like the time when he was recuperating from a heart attack and his doctor had him transported via a medical van to a rehabilitation clinic. The driver pushed my father's wheelchair up the ramp and into the van, secured the double doors, then proceeded to get into the van and drive away. What he forgot to secure, though, was my father's wheelchair! So at every stoplight, stop sign, or crosswalk, that van would come to a complete stop, but my father wouldn't. His wheelchair rolled all the way to the front of the van. Then, just as he was about to knock on the Plexiglas divider between the back area and the driver's seat, the driver would take off, sending my father rolling all the way to the back! The driver was oblivious to the roller derby of sorts that was going on behind him.

By the time they arrived at the rehabilitation center, my dad looked as though he had been through World War III! He was panting, his hair was in his face, and a couple of the buttons on his shirt had come undone. Dad had every right to yell at that driver, but he didn't. He simply waited until the driver opened the rear doors, then looked up through the hair falling down into his eyes and said, "That was better than a ride at Disneyland!"

I have plenty of fond memories of my mother, too. Memories that I determined I was going to make myself. I had spent many years wishing I could spend more time with my mother, but she worked full time and had four other children besides me, plus numerous grandchildren, with whom to divide her time. I knew she had always dreamed of seeing Washington, D.C., so one day I "kidnapped" her and we flew there. We had a great time, and now that she's gone, I'm so glad I didn't just sit around wishing I had more memories with her. I went ahead and created my own.

As you move through the grieving process, little by little you'll be able to let go of the pain and replace it with your memories. And memories are so much lighter and more enjoyable to carry.

Our losses in life
teach us to appreciate
the gifts that God gives.

Haiku by Diantha Ain

We do not remember days, we remember moments.

Cesare Pavese

While we are postponing, life speeds by.

Seneca

When They Leave Their Imprint on Your Life

Audrey was my mother's age. She had lived up the dirt road from my family for as long as I can remember. In the early days of my childhood, my family and hers explored life together. Whether it was marching up the long lane to the new neighbor's house as a pretend band, or sneaking into the house of Audrey's sister for a free lunch while she was gone, there were always plenty of adventures to be experienced together. Those were truly the good old days, when entertainment was simple and fun abounded in the least likely places. But time brings change, and sometimes that means drifting apart from beloved relationships.

As the years passed, so did the closeness once experienced between our families. On September 19, 1997, though, some unexpected tragic news brought us together again.

Upon returning home from a gospel concert late one night, I was informed by my parents that Audrey had been diagnosed with cancer. With today's advanced medical technology, there was hope that she could be cured. So, for the next eighteen months, Audrey bravely forged her way through two surgeries and continuous rounds of chemotherapy.

My mother and I made a weekly ritual of visiting her to show our love and support. I grew even closer to Audrey through those visits. Spending such precious time with her was an unexplainable joy. Her spirit and attitude were amazing. Even while battling for her life, Audrey was the hostess, never allowing Mom or me to leave without a snack. A few weeks before her death, while heavily medicated for pain, she even directed us to her homemade banana bread. Audrey was a giver. Not only did she unselfishly give away tangible things, but intangible ones as well—love, encouragement, joy, hope. No wonder everyone deemed her the Pollyanna of the neighborhood.

Audrey also instilled in me a love for fantasy and dreams. This was accomplished by her regular renditions of Shirley Temple's "Good Ship Lollipop" and Julie Andrews' "Supercalifragilistic-expialidocious." Her imagination, energy, and love of life were unmatchable. Audrey's favorite fantasy event was a tea party, and we had plenty of those, especially during the last few years of her life.

Laughter always occupied its rightful place in Audrey's home. She so preferred it to tears. I can remember sharing many laughs with Audrey while sitting at her kitchen table.

It's been almost two years now since Audrey lost her battle with cancer and was laid to rest in a quiet, country cemetery. I know that in the lives of those who knew her, her spirit lingers on. Her smile can still be seen, her laughter heard, and her unconditional love can still be felt. Beautiful people don't simply fade away and disappear. They may no longer dwell among us, but they've left their imprint on our lives. Audrey most certainly left one on mine.

Jessica Weisbrod

When You Don't Want the Memories to Fade

Grandma. I love that word. The mere mention of it floods my mind with happy memories—hugs, laughter, the toy cupboard, love, treats, surprises, anticipated visits, waving goodbye from the car window until Grandma's house is out of sight, and more hugs.

Alzheimer's. A word I don't totally understand and don't love at all. The dictionary defines Alzheimer's as "a degenerative disease of the central nervous system characterized especially by premature senile mental deterioration." Nice try, Webster. That tells me what is happening to my grandmothers medically, but it doesn't make it any easier for me to accept the daily changes.

Yes. I did say grandmothers.

My father's mother, known to me as Grandma Wood, is no longer here. She hasn't passed away physically, but her personality has left us. The grandma who once stitched intricate needlepoint, read Mary Higgins Clarke, and made the most delicious pies you'd ever want to eat is now a lady who shuffles incoherently around the seniors' home where she lives near us here in British Columbia, Canada. The most difficult thing for me is knowing that I can reach out and touch her hand, but I'll never again touch her heart.

My mother's mom, Grandma Rodgers, also doesn't remember who we all are anymore, but she wants to know. She asks my grandpa, "Who are they to me?" to try to fit the missing pieces into the puzzle of her memory. She can still give her famous hugs, and she cheers when something wonderful has happened. She knows how to laugh with us and love us, and even in her confused state, she can offer praise to God. She may not be able to bathe herself or do her own hair, she may even eat with her fingers, but she is still Grandma.

I thank God for both of my grandmothers, and I pray that they'll be with us for years to come. Losing a grandma to a disease like Alzheimer's is a different kind of loss. You lose them in stages, a little bit of them at a time. But while their memories are fading, I'm using this time to make memories of my own with each of them, memories that I hope I'll never ever forget.

Alzheimer's, a memory-maker instead of a memory-stealer? I wonder what Webster would have to say about that?

Aubrey Wood
Age 17

Keep praying, but be thankful that God's answers are wiser than your prayers.

William Culbertson

When You Didn't Want the Fun to Stop

I have written and rewritten a letter to my daughter, Anne, many times. To be honest, I dread all the things in life I have to face without my "little buddy." Grief sure is stinky. Days like this are hard to get through, but I usually end them by simply thanking God for allowing me to have raised Anne. So glad I was a part of her life. So glad that she was a strong Christian.

When Anne was unconscious on the ground on the athletic field and I was blowing my breath into her, and Loretta, a nurse I had just met, was performing CPR, all I could do was pray. At first the situation seemed surreal—like it wasn't really happening. Anne had been running laps when she suddenly collapsed that day. I told myself that she had simply fainted. She had fainted before. This was just another spell, and so, like I had always done before, I prayed for her to wake up.

As I began to realize that this time things were far more serious, my prayer changed. I begged God to let Anne live. She was so young, so full of life. Yet as each minute passed with still no response from Anne, my prayer began to change from "don't take her" to "take good care of her." At that moment I knew Anne was gone, and I was OK with giving her to God. I can't explain it, but there was a peace that came over me. Often, I have had to relive that moment to get through the depressing days that have followed.

Recalling fun memories with Anne has also helped. Anne and I shared so much laughter. Tell the "Cafeteria Lady" that I think of her a lot. Anne was emphatic about taking her own lunch to school every day. No matter how hard Ms. Pat, the cafeteria lady at Anne's school, tried, she could never talk Anne into eating school lunches. That's something I'm sure the Cafeteria Lady would understand.

If I could talk to Anne right now, this would be my message:

Dear Anne,

Thank you for being my daughter, friend, and treasure. I am so fortunate and blessed to have had you share your life with me.

I often think of all our many adventures—bowling, fishing, concerts, badminton, letter-writing, walking, homework, rodeos, and other happy times. Thanks for your many smiles and happy attitudes.

I must confess I still get sad when I walk in the house or look around school and am reminded that you are gone. I expect you to still be in your room, listening to music while writing your encouraging letters, or walking around campus with your many friends. The part of me that knows you are with God does rejoice. But when the sound of an ambulance goes by and your dogs start howling in mourning, our house seems so empty. Sometimes I want to go back and beg God to return you to me so we can resume our lives as they were. All these painful changes, so many at once, are a difficult reality to face.

I'm trying my best to adapt to this living without you. Routine is a comfort. Meeting new people brings the fear of uncomfortable conversations. I am very proud of you and I want to share the wonderful relationship you had and still have with God with others. Yet the emotions that arise with each question are painful, although I also know that talking about you and the loss I feel is ultimately healing. I am constantly relying on God to provide both my answers and the tissues.

I can tell you that the one thing that does keep me going is God's promise of eternity. I find comfort in looking for (and finding) His love all around me—in nature, in family and friends, in His Word, and in so many aspects of my daily life as I try to "keep on keeping on," as Grandma would say. God truly is my strength, as I know He was yours. I am so thankful, too, that because of His sovereignty I can know that I will see you again. I confidently count on His promises and I know that His heaven is more wonderful than I can imagine.

In conclusion, angel Anne, there is no conclusion. You will always be an important part of my life. I cherish my many memories of all the happy times we shared. Thank you, too, for your unyielding faith that came through so beautifully in your journals. Those journals, written for your own journey through this life, are now encouraging me.

Please thank God for the time that He allowed me to spend with you. I miss you so much and so anticipate the day when I'll be able to see you and never again have to say goodbye.

Love,
MooMa (Mom)

Raynette Farris

Never be afraid to trust an unknown future to a known God.

Corrie Ten Boom

A Step Toward Healing

Make or buy a notebook or journal and write down your memories of your loved one as you think of them. Be sure to include plenty of funny ones. Then, whenever you're feeling lonely, you can take out the book and relive your memories.

Find something to do this week in honor of your loved one. For instance, if he or she was a sports fan, offer to help out one of the coaches at your school. Or if he or she loved children, send an encouraging card to a sick child. Make your loved one's life count even more by doing something positive in his or her memory.

Chapter 21

Saying Hello to Healing

Your sun will never set again, and your moon will wane no more; the Lord will be your everlasting light, and your days of sorrow will end.

ISAIAH 60:20

There's nothing very good about having to say goodbye—especially when we weren't ready to say it. A friend or family member unexpectedly dies, a parent or sibling moves out of the house, a job transfer forces your family to relocate to a different part of the country—the scenarios for premature partings and reluctant farewells are countless. Whether we know they're coming, or they take us totally by surprise, goodbyes are never easy.

So why, then, do we have to say goodbye when we don't want to? The answer to this question is complicated, and it's one we might not fully understand until we get to heaven. In the meantime, we simply have to trust and believe that God's nature is loving and good, no matter what life throws our way.

One positive thing that comes from loss is that it makes the petty problems of everyday life pale by comparison. Suddenly, it doesn't matter who got the lead role in that school play, or whether or not we get that new CD. Loss gives us a new understanding of what's really important in life. It helps us get our priorities straight. Loss also intensifies our feelings. We find ourselves loving more deeply, laughing more heartily, and being more sensitive to the pain of others.

Still, there's no denying the fact that loss hurts. If you feel angry, bitter, and confused, not only is it your right to feel that way, it's healthy. For awhile. It means you're human, and you're working through the grieving process. The problem comes when you can't get past those feelings. You see only what you've lost, and are blinded to everything you still have. You focus only on the trials of your life, not on any of the blessings. If you're having trouble moving past those feelings, talk to someone—your parents, your minister, your teacher, a counselor, or a trusted friend. Don't grieve alone. There are people who want to help you, but you have to reach out.

The young people and adults in this book have all suffered loss. Terrible losses. They hurt just as much as you do. But they've survived, and they want you to know that you can survive, too. In fact, not only can you survive, you can make sure your loss counts for something. One way to do that is to help others who may be going through a similar loss. At the back of this book there is a list of organizations that could no doubt use your help. Talk to your parents about which one would be right for you to get involved with, or contact a local charity that might be able to use whatever talents you have to offer. Or think about someone in your life who is going through a loss. Why not reach out to that person with an encouraging word or a card? Remember how comforting a kind word was to you when you were going through your crisis? Pass along that kindness.

In closing, I hope this book has encouraged you in some way.

I hope it's shown you that you're not alone. Grief strikes all of us. It doesn't matter whether you're living in downtown Los Angeles or in rural Kansas, in England or Australia; it doesn't even matter if you're rich or poor, famous or not—none of us are immune. Yet we can make it through our grief with God's help and the help of our friends, family, and others who care.

It's not easy to think of new beginnings when a relationship, a life, or a situation has come to an end. Yet that's what each of these crises is. When someone we love dies or leaves us, it's a brand-new beginning for them. It can be a new beginning for us, too. It can be an opportunity to make better memories with those who are still with us, to not let those days and months pass without telling someone we love him or her. It can also be an opportunity to keep the memory of our loved one alive by becoming everything he or she wanted us to become. No, it's definitely not....

THE END

... it's a new beginning.

Learn from yesterday, live for today, hope for tomorrow.
Swedish proverb

Hotlines and Associations

You will be secure, because there is hope; you will look about you and take your rest in safety.

Job 11:18

The following is a list of organizations and hotlines that are available to you.

American Cancer Society
1599 Cliston Road NE
Atlanta, GA 30329
800-227-2345
www.cancer.org

American Cancer Society Camps (for children and families)
800-227-2345

American Diabetes Association
1701 North Beauregard Street
Alexandria, VA 22311
800-342-2383
www.diabetes.org

American Heart Association
National Center
7272 Greenville Avenue
Dallas, TX 75231
214-373-6300
800-AHA-USA1
www.americanheart.org

American Foundation for Suicide Prevention
888-333-2377

American Red Cross
P.O. Box 37243
Washington, DC 20013

Girls and Boys Town National Crisis Hotline
800-448-3000

Brave Kids (for kids with life-threatening illnesses)
www.BraveKids.org

Cancer Care Counseling
800-813-HOPE

Catholic Social Services
info@catholicsocialservices.com

City of Hope Hotline
1500 East Duarte Road
Duarte, CA 91010
800-852-8336 (Teenline)
www.cityofhope.org or cityofhope.com

Compassionate Friends (grief recovery)
www.thecompassionatefriend.org

Covenant House (24-hour hotline for kids at risk)
800-999-9999
(Also available in Spanish)

Foundation for the Children's Oncology Group
(Meredith Brucker, director of public affairs, raises money for
research for children and adolescents with cancer)
P. O. Box 60012
Arcadia, CA 91066
800-458-6223 ext. 198
www.nccf.org

Highlands Child Placement Center
5506 Cambridge Avenue
Kansas City, MO 64129
816-924-6565

International Association of Firefighters
NY Firefighters 9-11
P.O. Box 64858
Washington, DC 20035-5858

Leukemia and Lymphoma Society
800-955-4LSA

Locks of Love (takes donated hair for cancer patients)
888-896-1588
www.locksoflove.org

Mercy Ministries of America
Nancy Alcorn, President
P.O. Box 111060
Nashville, TN 37222-1060
615-831-6987
615-315-9749 Fax
mercymin@voy.net
www.mercyministries.com

National Runaway Switchboard
800-621-4000

National Youth Crisis Hotline
800-HIT-HOME

Ronald McDonald House
630-623-7048
www.rmhc.com

Salvation Army
Disaster Relief Fund for NYC
P.O. Box C-635
West Nyack, NY 10994-1739

The Samaritans (24-hour hotline, confidential)
212-673-3000

Teen Challenge
P.O. Box 1015
Springfield, MO 65801
417-862-6969
417-862-8209 (Fax)
tcusa@teenchallengeusa.com

United Way
701 N. Fairfax St.
Alexandria, VA 22314-2045
703-836-7100

Wigs for Kids (also takes donated hair for cancer patients)
440-333-4433

I expect to pass through this world but once. Any good thing, therefore, that I can do or any kindness I can show to any fellow human being let me do it now. Let me not defer nor neglect it, for I shall not pass this way again.

Stephen Grellet